FROM FAILURE TO SUCCESS

INDIGORIVER
PUBLISHING

FROM FAILURE TO SUCCESS

5 KEYS FOR PROFOUND CHANGE

ETHAN FISHER

KEYNOTE SPEAKER AND MENTAL HEALTH ADVOCATE

From Failure to Success: Five Keys for Profound Change

© 2024 by Ethan Fisher

Library of Congress Control Number: xxxxxxxxxx
ISBN: 978-0-xxxxxxx-x-x

Although this publication is designed to provide accurate information about the subject matter, the publisher and the author assume no responsibility for any errors, inaccuracies, omissions, or inconsistencies herein. This publication is intended as a resource, however, it is not intended as a replacement for direct and personalized professional services.

Editors: Marci Carson, Stephanie Thompson
Cover and Interior Design: Emma Elzinga

Printed in the United States of America

First Edition

3 West Garden Street, Ste. 718
Pensacola, FL 32502
www.indigoriverpublishing.com

Ordering Information:

Quantity sales: Special discounts are available on quantity purchases by corporations, associations, and others. For details, contact the publisher at the address above.

Orders by US trade bookstores and wholesalers: Please contact the publisher at the address above.

With Indigo River Publishing, you can always expect great books, strong voices, and meaningful messages. Most importantly, you'll always find . . . *words worth reading.*

THE PURPOSE OF THIS BOOK

L et me start out by saying that at no point throughout this book do I want *any* reader to think I put all the onus and blame on my mental health. Every choice I've made since I was old enough to think was of my own accord. I take full accountability for the destruction I've caused through the years. Denial is not a river in Egypt, but I still felt like I was drowning in it. For most of my life, I was unaware that I needed help. Like most people in denial, I made conscious and unconscious choices to not change. It's one hundred percent my fault— nobody else's. The few people who cared or even noticed my intense mood swings, alcohol binges, drug binges, and self-destructive actions rarely mentioned that I needed professional help. When the same few people did mention that I needed help, I chose not to listen, adhering to what many in denial do and avoided the conversation. And when that tough conversation took place, I would seek out entirely new groups of friends to dodge any possible such discussions. My entire focus and agenda in life was where I would play basketball, who I would drink with that night, and who would have drugs. Outside of those three wants in my life, nothing else really mattered. It was a sad existence, as my alcoholism and addiction were masking my underlying issues of untreated severe depression.

This book is divided into five sections that I built on to straighten out the course of my life.

PART 1: THE FOUNDATION

Your mental health, physical health, and financial health should be your priorities. These areas are the foundation of your life. It does not matter what life you lead—rich, poor, happy, or sad—your mental health controls everything in your body. Your mental health controls your energy, your moods, joy, happiness, fears, struggles, and pain. It's as simple as this: when you improve your mental health, your life improves. An improved mental health state will lead to less difficulty in your life. The healthier you are with your mental health, the more time and energy you will have to create a lasting impact with your loved ones, friends, and communities around the world. This eventually leaves more resources available for you to reach your full potential, or what you declare to be a successful life (Part 5). The "Foundation" section of the book tells my story, while Parts 2–5 include more data to back up my thinking.

PART 2: THE STRUGGLE

From the very moment we exit our mother's womb, we are faced with virtually insurmountable trials, tribulations, and struggles. Our first breath is a struggle. Eating is a struggle. We are born into a life with basically zero possibility of survival, yet approximately eight billion people currently live on this planet and have avoided death. *Nobody's* life is perfect and carefree. Chances are, if somebody tells you their life is perfect, they are flat-out lying. They are choosing to redact their struggles and pains with you. It's fine not to tell others about your struggles, but harboring them is often a root cause of cracks in your foundation

(Part 1). Even though some people appear as if they have it all figured out, more than likely they do not. Chances are they're struggling just as much as the next person—they are more skilled at hiding it or don't tell you how much it's really affecting them inside. They might briefly mention it and keep it moving forward. Some individuals are better equipped to compartmentalize their struggles than others.

When I'm struggling in life—which is often—it's likely due to the neglect of my own mental health and lack of the continuous maintenance of my foundation. The moment I act and address my struggles in my foundation (i.e., mental, physical, and financial cornerstones), my life seems to become easier to navigate. Throughout the first quarter-century of my life, I neglected everything that had to do with my foundation. Later in life, I finally learned how to avoid contributing to any large, catastrophic struggles in my life—although not all of them. I've learned to lessen many struggles, and in doing so, I decreased the length and duration of the minor struggles I faced. How? All by improving the different components of my foundation.

It's gut-wrenching to admit this, but from December 2020 through the summer of 2021, I did happen to lose my way. Toward the end of the COVID-19 pandemic's "emergency phase," something broke inside my brain, causing me to lose—for a time—my ability to stick to the game plan I've laid out in this book. Due to that fracture in my thought process, my life quickly fell apart. I lost everything that mattered to me except my sobriety, my career, and my dogs. I lost my wife to a divorce and my family to a fight. I lost my house, much of the stability that I had, and I came close to losing my career.

I'm slowly regaining my momentum by simply applying my own knowledge from the contents of this book. My life is already significantly better. Do I face struggles? Yes, of course. But I'm back on the path of improving my foundation, and things are becoming easier by the day. I'm living, walking proof that this system of mine works. I've proved it not just once, but many times over.

PART 3: THE FIVE KEYS

Life is not easy.

Part 3 is about the five keys for profound change that I use every day to remain focused on self-improvement and moving toward my life goals. These five simple keys will arm you with the necessary tools of resiliency and support you need moving forward. It's not always fun or glamorous, but the process and the ability to overcome struggles, no matter how big or small the struggle might be, will build a growth mindset. I live by these keys, which have been and are currently helping me through two of the worst moments in my life: the car accident in the past and my current divorce.

PART 4: LOVE AND VULNERABILITY

Do you love yourself? Weird question, right?

If you don't love yourself, how can you love others?

Everyone can greatly improve their reactions to all kinds of situations if they love themselves. If you dislike who you are and are unhappy with yourself, the "Struggle" (Part 2) will not be far behind. *But* once you learn to love yourself, your life will change for the better.

When you find true purpose in who you are and what you are all about, love will conquer. By learning to love with vulnerability, gratitude, and with intent, full purpose will lead you to loving yourself. Once you love who you are and have faith in who you are as a human being, the world becomes much easier to navigate. When you love your life, success follows—it's as simple as that.

PART 5: SUCCESS

"Success" will mean something different to every reader who picks up this book. What I do believe is this: if your long-term success seems to be floundering, chances are you are neglecting or missing something in the most important aspect of life—your foundation. I hate to beat a dead horse, but I feel so strongly about the foundation that I will often repeat it. If you are struggling, you can greatly improve your life by examining the foundational elements in Part 1. Then, if you use the five keys in Part 3 to address these cracks in the foundation, your life will improve. It won't be perfect by any means, but your life will be much better off.

You must check on your mental health because it might be preventing you from living a better, happier, and joyous life. I would know—I was stuck in Part 2, "Struggle," for many, many years, always hiding behind a bottle of booze or any substance that would numb my years, months, days—every minute of my life. This is no way to live, even if you have millions of followers and millions in the bank. Being happy, with a sense of purpose, is success. Part 4 talks about the truest form of success—"*love*," which brings about happiness.

CHAPTER 1

INTRODUCTION

You have a unique story. I have a unique story. Everyone on the planet has a unique story to tell. In my opinion, I believe that anyone and everyone can write a manuscript describing in detail what they've experienced, lived through, and learned. Anyone can write down and detail the tears of joy, pain, euphoric happiness, or the darkest depths of sadness one has lived through. Anyone can grace the page with stories from their ink quill. Life, the cruel bitch that she is, provides infinite knowledge—some good, some bad, and some with a dash of everything in between. There is a book in all of us. This happens to be my first and not the last.

Our experiences in life are based on the choices we make each moment of every day. We must realize our choices not only impact ourselves but every individual we encounter. You made a choice at this exact moment to put this book in your hands. You have a choice to stop reading right now (I hope you don't) or continue further. It will get interesting, I promise. Just think about how many hundreds of choices you made today to end up at this exact moment. There are so many different things you could be doing right now, but you are taking the time out of your day to read these words and stories. Thank you!

Fully aware of this, I want to provide you with information that can impact your life and impact the decisions you make. Over the years, I've learned the hard way from many of my struggles and deplorable mistakes. I've also learned from the positive successes of my choices as well. Many who have heard about my story or heard me speak seem to learn from both my poor choices on one hand, and on the other, are inspired by my positive outcomes from the rock bottom from which I have risen. Thousands of students, employees, coaches, and parents have reached out to me via email, text, or social media over the years, telling me about their stories in detail and how much they have learned from my story. Some of these messages have come years after they have seen me speak, highlighting the long-lasting effects my story and key-note presentations have had on them. That is why I'm spending count-less hours writing this book, which is another platform for me to reach inside your heart and your mind to help open your eyes to the power of your choices—and the devastation your poor decisions can have.

Let me get this out in the open right here, right now. I'm no differ-ent from you!

I've never taken an official IQ test. There is nothing special about me from an intelligence or physical standpoint.

More often than not, you will find me in long, baggy Jordan shorts, an old basketball t-shirt, or a sweatsuit hoodie. I will likely be wearing a baseball cap nearly covering my eyes with the brim intentionally low to block me from making eye contact with others. My social anxiety, while better than it used to be, plays a part in how often (or how little) I leave my house. When I'm comfortable in public, my hat is worn backward, especially when my alter-ego and self-confident attitude is out and I'm on stage speaking. No matter which way my hat is facing, it's covering up my widow's peak and my thinning, receding hairline, which I shave (by the way). The most distinguishing feature about me is my Romanesque soldier profile crooked nose. My nose is distin-guishable due to the five or six times it's been broken and reshaped, all from the hardened and sharp elbows caught from guys much taller than me on the basketball court. In years past, my college basketball program handouts listed me as a six-foot point guard. Ask my parents or family and they will quickly blurt out, "Don't listen to him; he's only five-foot-ten. I'm the one and only author of this book, so I will take the documented six-foot all day. But I'm not going to start off on a lie—I'm standing at a physically dominating five-foot-eleven frame, holding up a dad-like body, yet don't have any kids, so the dad body doesn't make sense. My ability to grow a nicely-shaped beard might cause some jealousy from those who can't, but overall, I'm an average man, just like much of the human population.

Right now, you are likely thinking, "Damn, why the heck am I taking precious time out of my day making a conscious choice to read this book?" You could be doing something fun, something exciting like bungee jumping or skydiving, instead of reading this ordinary guy's book.

Chances are, a few of you picked up this book due to its cover, which, to be frank—I had little to do with. Besides, I wrote that line before I even sent my first draft to the publisher. It's funny, but people pick books based on the cover versus the content, or at least I do most of the time. Chances are, the team of editors and designers took one of my ideas and combined it with those things called "psychology" and "science" to make my book stand out, hopefully catching as many eyes as possible. If that is your case, and you bought the book based on the cover, you meet the publisher's idea of the exact demographic and specific type of reader this book is aimed at selling to. Trust me, I had very little, if not zero, to do with that process to get you to this point. A few of you probably went to the back of the book, glanced over the short biography underneath my unique author picture, and instantly thought, "Why is this loser author wearing his hat backward? He appears to be older, grey in his beard. Shit, he must be going through a midlife crisis. Why are people paying him a lot of money to hear him speak? I've got to find out his story. Hell, maybe I can get paid big bucks to talk like him." Come back to this statement at the end of the book and see if you want to have a speak-off. I'll take you up on that challenge and win ninety-nine percent of the time!

I'll tell you right now what separates me from so many others. It's the same exact characteristic that most, if not all, successful people have. Have you ever watched interviews or read books on successful athletes, entrepreneurs, entertainers, and musicians like Richard Branson, LeBron James, Albert Einstein, and thousands of other successful people? The secret can't be determined by standardized tests to get you into the Ivy League schools. Those tests can and will help, but are not necessary (i.e., Bill Gates, Mark Zuckerberg) to be successful. What they all obtain can't be measured from an IQ or EQ test. It cannot be measured by trainers at professional sports combines or a pre-draft workout—it cannot be improved by lifting weights and studying harder.

Here's the secret!

Many of the successful outwork, out-hustle, and out-grind every one of their peers who are chasing the same exact dreams that they had. The successful wanted to succeed more than their colleagues and peers. They wouldn't accept being average. They all have an internal *desire* to be better than everyone else. Each one of them possessed a purposeful belief and faith in themselves. An internal fire that ignited their energy and passions, allowing them to outwork anyone standing in their path to their audacious goals and dreams. Belief and faith in themselves! A purposeful desire to persevere through any roadblock on their way to big, audacious goals. That is what separates average people from the greats. If you have these types of traits, you don't need my help or others' help to succeed. Mind you, having a life coach, business coach, and/or trainer will increase your efficiency and increase the level of success you will have. Here's the *but*, a big *but*. If you lack these simple traits above, little else matters in your road to success.

What has separated me from many during this journey from failure to success? A desire, drive, determination, and heart that will never stop—a never-quit philosophy of bend-but-not-break mindset. You need to be an ambitious, audacious goal chaser, layered with a *belief* in self that nobody else can see. That is what separates me from others. I'm willing to lose everyone in this process because I'm selfish in what I want and what I desire to accomplish in life. Do I have regrets? Yes, but I will not stop until I reach my goals. I will plow through everything in my way! When you find that internal fire fueled and ignited by life experiences, with unmatched levels of perseverance and resiliency and a drive to succeed, *nothing* will stop you—except yourself! You must be willing to never quit, never give up on the goals you set. It's as simple as that. Those who are successful are those who never quit on their belief and faith in themselves. They never stopped moving forward toward their end-goals.

You will read stories throughout this book describing multiple moments where I had the option to quit. It would have been easy to chase new goals, and it would have been much easier to change paths in life. My desire was to thrive against all odds, to prove everyone wrong, to prove to myself I was never a quitter, no matter how bleak the future looked. I had doubters and haters who watched and whispered, some even yelling their thoughts about me out loud. "Ethan is a has-been, a nobody." I picture all you scrub-ass mother fuckers every time I speak on my "Desire" slide in my keynote presentations. Thirty-plus years later, I'm still motivated by little remarks and quotes from people who doubted me in high school, who doubted me in college, and those who doubted me recently. The fire is ignited into flames when I think about every person who doubted me, stabbed me in the back, talked shit, or thought less of me. I fucking love it!

I want to win, period. I want to be the best at whatever goal I focus on. I'm competing against myself with a laser aimed at every top keynote speaker, motivational speaker, and self-proclaimed top youth speaker in my way. I'm competing every day to be better at my career as a speaker. Inside of me grows a "dawg," a competitive spirit boosted with levels of anger and intensity to prove everyone wrong. I'm a vicious dawg, willing to fight to the death if need be.

Do you have the positive, anger-filled intensity and aggression coursing through your blood when people, including mentors, tell you it's time to change professions? Do you have that same intensity when those closest to you say they have your back but show that they don't believe in you anymore? I do! That is what separates me from the masses. It's not my IQ, my EQ, my skill, or my talent. It's a burning desire inside that separates others from the masses. The greats are great because they have an unwavering belief in themselves.

Before you read any further, I want to address a few things. This book was *not* written to sugarcoat life. In my opinion, sugar-coating doesn't benefit anyone. Life is not easy. Life will be hard on everyone and even harder on some than others. Those with the right attitude and focus can learn how to navigate the choppy waters of life using the teaching points in this book.

My life isn't perfect by any stretch of the imagination, but it's certainly a heck of a lot better than where it was in the past and where it could be. Every day I wake up with the intent to improve, attempting to become a better man than I was the day before. Yes, there are many days, weeks, and even months where I struggle. There are many days where the darkness that once haunted me as a teen comes back around, an uninvited knocking on my front door, just waiting for my subconscious to let the defeatist attitude lay anchor with its weight of depression and darkness again.

I've hit rock bottom multiple times, coming back from the depths of despair and darkness victorious, not once or twice but many times. If I can recover, so can you. Much of my rock-bottoms came from my untreated mental health issues, which is not a weakness. Mental health is a legitimate issue that, in many cases, will have to be battled day in and day out. It takes massive amounts of energy, strength, and power to keep fighting. My knuckles are bloody from swinging my fists and fighting on and off for the last three decades. My strength to battle depression with calloused and hardened battle hands has given me the ability to grip onto tools and use them as a defense against these demons of mental health, alcoholism, and drug addiction. I've garnered battle-tested experiences to fight for every breath in this life.

In a few chapters, I will describe how I pictured ending my life. There will be a head's up at that point, so you can skip it if that is a healthy choice for you. I chose to include such a detailed description because it portrays a real-life moment when my mind went into the void of darkness. It's meant to be alarming, it's meant to be scary, and it's meant to bring awareness to those who are lucky and don't know how somebody's mind works at a time of crisis. There are countless others who struggle with similar thoughts but differ from mine depending on their own experiences. This is me—the good, the bad, the ugly, and everything in between.

Written in these pages is my heart, my emotions. They contain sad stories, and they contain the positive five keys that will help you out of tough times, as they continually do for me. My hope is to flood your thoughts, altering the choices you make moving forward. There's a quote I repeat often, although I can't take credit for it, as I picked it up along my journey: "Pressure busts pipes…or it can make diamonds." The first person to tell me this was a friend named Tino. He would follow that with a "foo." What outcome in life are you going to choose? Are you going to choose to be a busted pipe, leaking gas or liquid into the air or on the ground? Or are you going to be battle-tested, forged with pressure, and turn your life into a diamond? I know the choice I made and will continue to make. You might not think it, but it is a choice. Life is filled with choices, so choose wisely!

CHAPTER 2
THE OLD ME

Before October 2004, I was a bum and a complete loser, a nobody going nowhere but to an early grave. I wouldn't want anyone's kids to emulate me. Life was spent walking around in a dream state. Grandiose visions filling my head with truckloads of dollars, somehow magically filling my bank account with commas and zeros—allowing me to travel the world and live a rich and famous, carefree, stress-free life. How would I earn these dream millions? Duh—basketball. I was going to play professional basketball. Let's just say I was not in touch with reality. Let's be real. I had more of a chance to win the state lottery than playing in the National Basketball Association (NBA).

My mind played tricks on me. As a fictitious illusion from a supremely overconfident, delusional mind, I truly believed I could play at that level and would make it one day. Even more ridiculous than that dream to make it to the NBA were my actions. I was under the false reality that I could ingest copious amounts of alcohol and mind-altering substances and still make it. I wanted to party like a rap star but play professional basketball. Frankly, the two don't mix.

It's perfectly okay to dream big. I want every reader to have large aspirations, even if you are the only one who can see them. It's important to have big dreams and visions at any age. The problem with my audacious goals wasn't the dream itself, it was the work ethic and the choices I made, which were followed by continuous screw-ups. I never had a game plan. I never made a commitment to 4 a.m. workouts or two-a-days like my friends who played professionally overseas. Not once did I execute a workout routine that would create an opportunity to chase the unlikely 0.05% dream of playing in the NBA. I know I could have played overseas, even had a chance to at the age of thirty-four, but due to my past choices, my dream was never brought to a reality.

Playing basketball was all I wanted to do as a kid. It was in the fourth grade, after watching the VHS tape called *The Pistol*, when I began dribbling between my legs around the cul-de-sac with the intent of not messing up. That movie changed my life. It highlighted the unreal talent and dedication "Pistol Pete" Maravich had as a young boy. He was driven by his father to be the best that he could be. Pistol would ride his bicycle while dribbling a ball on the way to school, something I tried but never conquered at an early age. For me, the love and passion for the game with an orange bouncing ball was there from the beginning. So, this fourth grader believed he could be the next Pistol. Looking back, I believe even more in what could have been my destiny if not for adolescence, mental health issues, alcohol, and substance abuse, which destroyed any potential work ethic I had as a child.

What I lacked was not the love or the passion for the game of hoops. What was needed and required was the ability to realize I was in control of my own life. The older I became, I more allowed *my own* self-defeating attitude and mindset of a punk-ass adolescent teen with an "I don't give a fuck" attitude to control my future. I was an angry teen—so confused, depressed, scared, and stubborn. Lacking any semblance of reality about what it would take to make my dreams come true, I fucked up my life. In the process of doing so, I ended up ruining other people's lives as well. That's what hurts the most still to this day.

Life quickly became unmanageable when my mind began telling me lies. My lost soul felt the need to turn into a "bad boy" to garner attention from others. This adolescent angst to influence friends began negatively influencing my choices. Regrettably, I was feeding an insatiable appetite for large quantities of liquor, drugs, music, and basketball. The cornerstones in my life shifted from an innocent kid's dream to play ball to an enraged, shy, zit-faced teen consumed by lying to others and indulging in alcohol and weed and the hip-hop/rap culture of the Fab Five, Allen Iverson, and Tupac. As a skinny, zero-muscle skeleton of a teen, I felt instantly powerful with a basketball dribbling and my headphones blaring. This newfound pseudo-confidence, mixed with a very high blood alcohol content, caused my reality and over-inflated ego to come crashing down. If I only knew what these destructive behaviors would lead to years later, I would have stopped in a heartbeat. But we all know that life only moves forward, never backward, no matter how hard you wish and pray. This thing called life continues moving toward the future—never the past. I'd do everything over if I could, and everything changed on the worst imaginable night of November 9, 2003.

CHAPTER 3
LIFE CHANGED IN AN INSTANT

The game plan was to drink with some friends that I hadn't seen since I came home from my fifth attempt at playing college basketball. One of the friends called to say he was housesitting and there was a hot tub and a spare bedroom for me to stay in for the night. After listing the names of about eight to nine people I knew and was comfortable around, he said, "Come by and see some of your friends who you haven't seen in months." At the time, my friend knew I was isolating from people, and he knew I didn't like going to the bars anymore. Besides, he knew I was drinking at home solo anyway, so why not spend some time with friends?

Giving in, I decided to go to the small house party.

I went with the plan to stay the night with no intention of going anywhere else. I was going to drink, play cards, and maybe score with one of the single ladies that would be there. Then I'd get up the next morning with a splitting headache and massive hangover, eat some breakfast, talk about the night, and go home to my parents' house. This was a typical weekend night for a college student, nothing out of the regular. Yet alcohol and good decisions are never synonymous with each other. One of the many negative side-effects of alcohol includes making irrational decisions based on emotional reactions, never leaving the drinker thinking clearly. At some point during the night, my cerebral cortex shut off from the amount of alcohol I consumed, leaving me in an altered, blackout-drunk state.

Months later there would be written testimonies and witness statements describing me as "acting off" and "very unusual." At one point during the alcohol-induced blackout, I jumped, fully clothed, into the hot tub. In the testimonials, this was mentioned as "out of the norm" since everyone else was prepared with bathing suits and towels. Not me—I couldn't conform to the conventional method of changing into a pair of swim shorts. Instead, with my blood coursing with Carlo Rossi strawberry wine, I had to make a spectacle of myself and do the opposite of the other party goers, jumping fully clothed into the hot tub. Witnesses said that I went downstairs shortly after the hot tub event to change into some dry, clean clothes.

Nearly twenty-four hours later, my eyelids opened and nothing made sense. I was confused, lost, and questioning, *Where am I? What am I doing in here?* Once my mind began to work again, I instinctively grabbed the side of the bed, ready to jump to the floor and get the heck out of the strange room. Before my waist could break free from the bed, I felt a tight resistance on my mid-section. I ran my hands in between my legs and noticed a tube inserted into my body. I quickly fumbled up the length of the plastic tube until I lost it entering my own flesh. I pulled, writhing in extreme pain, as little drops of fluid hit my fingertips. I quickly realized I had a catheter tube inserted inside me and I couldn't get it out. Panicking with nowhere to go, I closed my eyes tight, wishing this was just a nightmare and I would wake up from this scene.

The truth about my situation was about to hit me, and it would be a real-life nightmare, not some dream. With all my might, I began trying to recollect how I ended up at this point.

The first nurse I spoke to asked me, "Mr. Fisher, do you know what happened last night?" After I shook my head in bewilderment, the nurse politely said, "It wasn't good." Then she proceeded to check on my vitals before walking out of the room.

My mind began to race even more. What transpired? Why was I here? Panic set in.

A second nurse entered the cold, dark hospital room and asked me the same question. "Do you know what you did last night?"

With what I can only assume was a confused, terrified, and puzzled look, I shook my head and gave her a soft, "No."

What came out of her mouth destroyed me.

"You drunk drove and killed somebody."

Lying in that hospital bed, my thoughts began bouncing faster than atomic particles being slingshot through the tunnels of CERN. Reality began burning and scorching my neuropathways, creating a memory destined to cause a lifetime of pain and scars. It was as if an Amtrak train turned the corner at full speed and fell off the track—before turning into a fiery ball of death and destruction. I was confused and utterly lost. All I could think about were the dark clouds circling within my mind. Hours passed. I randomly shook my head and thought it would all disappear—it would be just one of those damned alcohol-induced, vivid nightmares. That kind of nightmare never came, and the realization of what materialized became *real*.

After hours in the darkness, through the uncontrollable sobbing, my mind began forming thoughts about what to do. After years of incurring brain damage from the alcohol, drugs, and depression, I still had enough gray matter to begin evaluating what would end up being three distinct options for the next steps in my life. Facing a crossroad that I would wish on no living human, I was about to make choices in that hospital bed that could determine who I might become years later.

The first coherent thought that popped up into my frontal lobe…

RUN

My initial thought: *You've been running away your entire life. You're not handcuffed to the bed—run before it's too late.*

My heart began to beat faster, my blood flowed at a greater velocity, and I began thinking about all the places I could run to. A few of my friends lived in other countries, some of who played professional basketball. My instinct was to run away and live with one of them. It was something I had talked about doing anyway—now I had a very serious reason to do so. Running away had legitimate appeal. Then I thought of my little brothers and my mom and dad. The reality of never seeing them again shook me to my core. Then the second option hit me...

SUICIDE

I began thinking, *Die, E. Die. Just fucking kill yourself and end this pain. Stop being a pussy and do it.* My inner voice was pleading repeatedly, *End the pain before reality takes place. Hurry up and kill yourself.*

In bed with my head in my hands, I was hunched over, sobbing while my mind was screaming, *What have you done?*

I had a sudden urge to pray. Scared to death, hands shaking with fear, an overwhelming something took over. I couldn't tell you exactly what it was, but it was as if a thousand words pierced my eardrums at once, cyphering one distinct concept, and an urge came over me to...

TAKE RESPONSIBILITY

I can't explain anything that ensued, but at that moment I had to change. It was as if God answered my prayers. At that moment, without any prior relationship with God, He spoke to me, influencing or speaking life into the rock-bottom situation I had just created. Nothing has been the same since that moment in my life.

This book is not a memoir about my life, as it was originally planned to be. This book has grown into something much more substantial and practical. Starting with the simple question, "Are you okay?" (Chapter 5). Asking "Are you okay?" is a foundational brick to help make people's lives better and such a simple yet substantial question we should all ask ourselves and others. I truly believe if I could have addressed my problems in middle school, I might not have turned to alcohol and drugs to mask my mental health situation. I might have changed if one college coach would have had a heart-to-heart with me and asked, "Are you okay?"

I've learned over the years that mental health is the foundation of anyone's life. Millions struggle every day. This book is another way to provide stories and services to those who are struggling to find their way, just like I was and still am today. Wait a second. Did I just say I still struggle? Yes, you are correct. I still struggle today with my manic depression and social anxiety disorder, but I've learned how to manage my life for the most part (minus the end of the pandemic), and now I'm significantly better than I was before I hit rock bottom at seventy-two miles per hour.

This is the great thing about life. No matter who you are, the background you come from, or how you were raised, *we can all change.* We, you, me, all of us can change this very second. Yes, you can change from the moment you are reading these words. That empowers me as I write and edit this paragraph. It starts an internal desire to change and believe in yourself and nobody else. Nobody can do it for you. It is all on you! If I can fundamentally change my desire to live, serve, and inspire, anyone else can.

It starts right now, with *one choice* to change your entire life!

What choice will you make? Are you going to change your life?

PART 1

THE FOUNDATION

Most business owners, doctors, lawyers, teachers, or any other workplace professionals have one thing in common: they all lacked a depth of knowledge and particular expertise in their occupations when they first started out. Brilliant computer programmers and coders who create complex algorithms all started with elementary basic math: 1 + 1 = 2. These coders began with the basics, building layer upon layer of learned proficiency until they could create complex, seemingly living and breathing algorithms. Granted, many are beyond exceptional with abnormally high IQs, but the point is, even they started with the basics of math like the rest of us.

Michael Jordan, arguably the greatest professional NBA basketball player ever, didn't calmly walk on the basketball court, jump a few feet in the air with a basketball, and dunk the ball on his first try. As a matter of fact, Michael "Air" Jordan was cut from the high school team his freshman year because he wasn't skilled or tall enough to beat out the upper classmen in varsity basketball. Unlike many in Jordan's situation, he didn't go home and sulk in a corner like most of us would have done. He didn't give up. Instead, he made a choice to continue on, followed by countless more small decisions that would alter the course of his life and history. Jordan devoted his life to making the varsity basketball team and being the best player that he could be. He didn't just wish for it to happen, he went out and began improving on the basics of the game. He worked on his footwork, pivots, jab steps, layups, and the fundamentals that are the foundations of the game. Jordan worked tirelessly on his foundations to become the Jordan we all know today. After countless hours of practice, Jordan made his high school team the following year—and the rest is history. Jordan doesn't become synonymous with the "Greatest of All Time" (GOAT) conversations or become the first black athlete to become a billionaire without making the small choices essential to his foundations daily. He chose to be the MJ we all know and hear about by never giving up and making choices every day to move forward on his path to success.

Have you ever found yourself standing on the top floor of a gigantic skyscraper, hundreds of feet in the sky, tentatively placing one foot in front of the other, nervously looking at the window and floor, making sure there is no possible way to free-fall hundreds of feet to your imminent death? Ever wonder how these magnificent towers stand so tall and so firm yet can gently sway back and forth, standing strong against the natural elements? They robustly handle the Earth's weather conditions, ranging from lightning strikes and snowstorms to massive hurricanes. I'm far from a structural engineer, but what I do know about skyscrapers is they are not built from the top floor first and finished at the basement parking garage.

Architects and teams of engineers begin planning the building years before they break ground. The building schematics are meticulously planned down to the centimeter before any brick is laid and before you can see the panoramic view and curvature of the earth from the 101st floor. For a few moments, you are engulfed by the world's beauty, forgetting just how high up in the sky you are and that this amazing man-made structure was built by the basics of math, science, and human education in architectural design engineering.

Where do these massive concrete high-rises begin—how do they start? At the very bottom, and not the ground layer, or the first floor that we can all see with the naked eye. These gigantic buildings start hundreds of feet deep into the earth, creating a fortified, solid foundation before one length of rebar is even laid down for construction.

Without the appropriate building materials, a steel frame, and hundreds of structural engineers and architects, the building will likely tumble and fall—injuring, if not killing, thousands of lives. When designing a building, the most important component of the building is the foundation.

The same process should be applied to a person. Our foundation is our brain. The human brain is the most amazing, complex, and powerful living supercomputer in the universe. If we don't take care of our brains, including our emotional, psychological, and physical health, we are in for a bumpy ride. We need to start focusing more attention and time on these things to achieve lasting success.

It is completely normal human behavior to have feelings. Being sad is okay; being anxious is okay. Struggling from a breakup with your significant other is difficult, and finding yourself in the dark, sobbing uncontrollably in pain is okay. To feel that way, allowing the tears to fall like waterfalls, is okay. Did a pet die? Did you lose a job? Argue with a family member or close friend? All of these are common human interactions and situations. It's completely normal to feel pain and mourn when we are sad or lonely. There is nothing wrong with having feelings, whether angry, distraught, exhausted, tired, or sad. Humans are emotional beings. What's not okay is when those feelings begin to prevent you from experiencing life. That is when you need help.

One of my goals in this book is to break down the stigma of mental health. I personally have used counseling on and off since 2004. It's perfectly healthy to seek help and treatment. This book is one of my platforms to explain the necessity of getting help. I want mental health to be looked at like athletes who seek trainers. If you sprain an ankle or think it might be broken, where do you go? You go to a trainer or doctor. The same should be said for mental health. If you have a brain sprain (anxiety or depression), go to a doctor and get help. It's that simple! The ambition behind my public speaking is a desire to normalize the whole topic of mental health—and the growing number of mental health advocates out there is helping this conversation even more. We are trying to bring about awareness to the masses and educate those who think they are alone in this battle. We are all trying to make those struggling realize and understand that they are not alone. Millions, if not billions, of people struggle every day. You are not alone.

CHAPTER 4
YOU ARE NOT ALONE

Maya Angelou said, "I've learned that people will forget what you said, people will forget what you did, but people will never forget how you made them feel." I am a story-telling preventative keynote speaker who makes audiences cry with my honest depictions of pain and trauma. I also make them laugh at the joyful moments in my life. Attendees generally look inward, reflecting on the choices they've made and will continue to make. The audience might never remember my name or be able to recall major details of my story, but I've made an imprint on their souls and spirits that will often last a lifetime. It is a goal of mine to speak with such passion that they *never* forget that moment when they cried in a gym packed with their classmates or at a conference with their coworkers over some keynote speaker's story. They will remember how I made them feel.

The validation of services I perform often comes out in the individual conversations with audience members after my events. Most of the time, the situation goes like this: "Mr. Fisher, can we talk, alone or privately, please?" with fear and trepidation oozing out of their bodies. "I'm sorry. I don't want to be a burden," as they continue to whisper, thinking that their classmates or coworkers, also waiting in line, will hear anything that comes out of their mouths. My reply is always along the lines of, "No problem. Of course. What's up?" with a curious, inquisitive tone. My eyes quickly begin seeking out a member of the administration or staff, making sure I get eye contact followed by a tiny nod of approval when dealing with a school-aged student. With an adult, it's easier—we step outside of the room and into the hallways. In either case, the student or adult is unburdening their personal stories of childhood trauma, family issues, divorce, death, their failures, suicidal ideation, or worse—they talk about a person close to them that was lost by alcohol, a drug overdose, or a completed suicide. A large portion of these stories are concerning, leaving me feeling somber inside, but I must display strength and keep my senses about me.

Everyone deserves my undivided attention, especially when their shoulders are slumped, their eyes are looking at the ground, and their body is nervously swaying back and forth. It is a must that I pay attention to the individual's position and the angle of their feet. A lot of the time, their feet are not directly pointed at me but turned sideways toward the exit doors. They are ready to flee at any given moment, anticipating a sprint to the door before they gain enough strength to tell me their story. A number of these individuals have better physical form than Olympic gold medalist Usain Bolt at the starting blocks, anticipating the starting gun about to go off. So far, I've never spoken with a "sprinter." They all eventually let their guard down, expressing something in their life that has been buried and burning inside for as long as they can remember.

I say something brief in a firm yet soft tone as the coach in me comes through, making sure they see the strength and vulnerability in my eyes as if saying, "I'm here to help you; you are safe with me." It's very important they see into my eyes. They need to see the sincerity and warm embrace from the windows of my soul. They need to feel safe and secure. They need to feel this way promptly so I can persuade them to open up as quickly as possible due to the limited time I have with each person.

All a student wants is for an adult to listen and take them seriously.

Most of the adults they come in contact with are consumed by their own grown-up responsibilities, often not paying attention to the young person who is struggling right in front of them. The student is seeking validation—they want somebody to listen to their stories. They want to feel important. More importantly, they want to feel seen. Being young is difficult. On top of that, being young in a world that places so much value on superficial social media influence is even harder to imagine. The young can quickly get lost in the millions of popular posts, pictures, tweets, and snaps of that day. All they really want is to feel valued. Heck, that's what most humans want. We all want to feel valued and important. No matter the age demographic of the audience, my job is to convey that they "are not alone" in the feelings they are dealing with inside.

It's not always the sad, sorrowful stories I hear. Often, it's a group of individuals showing unbridled joy and excitement, speaking so fast I can barely understand them. They are so excited to finally have somebody to talk to about the challenges they've overcome or how the speech inspired or motivated them. To me, this is the greatest feeling in the world. I had no idea that a storytelling, motivational, inspirational, preventative keynote speaker—or however you want to describe what I do—would impact so many lives and be this amazing and awesome.

In life, there is always yin and yang, a give and a take, a light and a dark. Being a preventative storytelling speaker is no different—this job comes with difficulties and drawbacks. With a little over five hundred events in my rear view and growing, the drawbacks are much more difficult than I realized at first. It's very rare that I don't have an individual break down in front of me, crying their eyes out and, in between sobs, explaining their personal or even family difficulties with anxiety, alcohol abuse, cutting, depression, sexual abuse, substance abuse, trauma—and more times than I want to admit, suicidal ideation. I've received thousands of emails, texts, or DMs from audience members days, weeks, even years later, as they finally have the strength to voice their individual trauma. It can be extremely tough to deal with all of this, but the biggest takeaway I've gathered over the years is: we are all struggling. The youth, mothers, fathers, coaches, and employees from low level to C-suite are struggling. The global pandemic in 2020 created more issues in this world than we could have been prepared for. Out of the struggle of 2020–2021, I've forced myself to take away something positive from the twenty-four-plus months of the pandemic.

Yes, I found one positive takeaway, and here it is.

The world can now relate to and understand what it's like to face struggles involving anxiety, depression, isolation, and the feeling of being lost or alone. I think nearly every person walking the earth faced some type of struggle during the pandemic.

I believe the world currently understands that we all need a shoulder to cry on, an ear to pour our isolated, dark thoughts into. I know I need somebody to do that with. Life is difficult, no matter who you are or where you come from. Isolation from family and friends is a horrible experience that billions of people lived through and experienced during the COVID-19 crisis. It was a form of prison on a global scale, with people missing family holidays, birthdays, weddings, and funerals due to concerns about their own mortality. Anyone who follows the news knows that millions of people lost their jobs, becoming financially destitute while locked in tiny apartments with kids and little-to-no entertainment. Alcohol sales, substance abuse, divorce, and domestic violence increased, the last two often stemming from the first two. As we all know, it wasn't just a few grueling days, weeks, or even months. It lasted nearly two-and-a-half years, and many experts say much of that unresolved trauma from lockdown will continue for years to come.

TIME TO END THE STIGMA

For generations, mental health has been stigmatized by the media and the masses. The world has been influenced for decades by newspapers, magazines, and water cooler conversations at work. News outlets have often publicized mental health issues as weakness, showing their audiences that a person with mental health issues will not be able to function or make it in the real world. Talking about anxiety, depression, or stress has been taboo—often making people uncomfortable when hearing those words. If any of those mental health issues were mentioned or associated with a particular person, they were likely to become outcasts, not only to family and friends but in the community as well. When an individual mentioned they were struggling with mental health, they were sometimes labeled "crazy" or "unstable." The foundations of why those individuals were struggling in the first place, the failure of realizing there is a root cause to mental health problems, which is likely to be some childhood, teen, or adult trauma—have not been properly addressed.

Fear tends to control the narrative around polarizing topics such as mental health. Individuals with their own insecurities or poorly educated histories would create falsified stories about those who previously opened up about their internal struggles with anxiety, depression, and other mental health issues. Individuals who admitted to mental health issues were often referred to psychological institutions, labeled, and placed in a psych ward—or what kids in my day used to call a "loony bin"—adding fuel to the burning negative flame of mental health. All of this perpetuated the negative connotation and perception of someone's mental health.

Maybe that was just my upbringing and the way people looked at mental health in the 1980s and 1990s in northern Colorado. It sounded scary to me and was the sole reason I never told anyone I was struggling. Plus, I didn't want to be bullied or treated like an outcast. In school, I was already struggling with puberty, girls, and social settings—adding a "crazy" label would have driven me even further into the darkness. That is why I tell audiences now I certainly wouldn't want to grow up in this generation with all the social media pressures—I was ready to take my own life in the eighth grade when cell phones and social media weren't invented yet. I can't fathom what kids are dealing with now. The types of peer pressure that exist today cause individuals to fear talking about their struggles. Social media has made "perfection" the unattainable standard, so young people fail to realize that even the best and most popular people struggle. *Nobody is perfect*—we all struggle with something.

I FELT ALONE; I FELT CRAZY

When I was growing up, the stigma surrounding mental health was nothing like it is today. "Mental health" wasn't even a term to describe mental health. Anyone who had a mood disorder or chemical imbalance in the brain, like anxiety or depression, would be seen and called out as weaknesses. Very few talked about the issues or personal mindsets going on inside. I know I felt like I was the only one in the world that had these dark thoughts and swinging moods, often telling myself, *I'm the worst. I'm a loser. Nobody can feel as bad as I do. I have to be the only one feeling like this.* With these negative thoughts ruminating over and over, leading me to question my own insanity, my constant internal voice was saying, *Maybe I am crazy. Why is this happening to me? Am I crazy? I feel crazy. I hope nobody knows or sees this.* My internal thoughts and dialogue were scary. There was no way I would tell anyone, so I tried to maneuver through life alone thinking I was a weirdo/crazy person. I kept this fear locked inside, never daring to let anyone know about it because of the shame and embarrassment it would bring into my world.

Back then, we were conditioned to believe that kids who were different were crazy or weird. In elementary and middle school, my independent thought process had yet to take shape. My adolescent, impressionable brain was soaking up everything I heard, inadvertently being trained through random words, far-fetching rumors, and lies spewing out of other kids' mouths. I was young and dumb, and the negative bias toward other kids who were "weak" or "crazy" planted its roots deep into my own programming. I'd often hear other kids talk badly about somebody who was struggling. Kids being kids, unconsciously and without understanding, would often blurt out and even scream, "They are crazy. They should be in a loony bin." These verbal outbursts ultimately planted the seed of fear about the future issues I would have. Hearing these things as a kid who was still struggling with learning to color within the lines—something I still struggle with—I was involuntarily picking up defective thinking.

During my very rough sophomore year in high school, one of my best friends called me weird. That moment left me feeling self-conscious and even defensive to this day. Internalizing that word at the age of fifteen, I apathetically retreated inward, making sure not to act out or be "me" because I didn't want to be thought of as a weirdo by my other friends. Looking back on that moment, I know she didn't mean to hurt me, but the way my brain processed the information began changing the direction of my future just one simple degree at a time. You don't realize the small, incremental moments that begin to change your life until you reflect on them later, trying to learn from your situation to help others experiencing those same moments.

That one degree of change might not seem like much, but take the stock market, for example, and the topic of compounding interest. If you earn just one percent per year, it might not seem worth paying attention to, but left alone, that one percent becomes two percent the following year and three percent the year after. It compounds, and then you are looking at a gigantic change in your investments over a ten, twenty, or thirty-year span. Quickly and silently, I stopped acting like me, changing one percent in my sophomore year and two percent in my junior year. By the time I hit twenty-three years old, I had shifted by almost double digits into a different person. The way I handled my new self also shifted. Even now, when I'm relaxed and comfortable with somebody, I'm a goofball, but only a select few know that. Most people think I'm quiet, uptight, and mean. The comfortable weirdo has been hidden from the world since I was fifteen when I began being less open to showing people who I really was.

WE ALL NEED HELP

Over the years, I've been speaking to our youth, hoping to change their entire lives by talking in-depth about the topic of mental health. Something also needs to happen in the corporate workspace where avoiding, hiding, and shunning mental health issues has been the norm for way too long. Employees have been programmed and trained to never speak openly about their personal issues at the job site. The moment an employee steps foot on the business property, they are paid to work, follow the rules and guidelines, and then go home and discuss their personal life outside of business hours. To climb the ladder, you need to hold mental health issues in, show up to work even when you're sick, and perform until your work is finished. Only then can you go home and have a good cry.

Before the pandemic, it was reported that over twenty percent of the U.S. population was struggling with a mental health issue,[1] and society has programmed us to hide those issues deep inside. That number has nearly doubled (thirty-three percent) since the pandemic.[2] Think about it—nearly thirty-three percent of the U.S. population. In other words, more than 100 million people in the USA alone are struggling. This does not take into account the nearly eight billion additional individuals living in other parts of the world. How many billions struggled during the pandemic and continue to struggle now? I cannot express this enough, but if you are struggling, it is okay because *you are not alone* in this fight with mental health.

Holding issues inside can become destructive to the individual—impacting their daily lives—but from an economic standpoint, it ends up hurting the bottom line of a company's profit due to loss of productivity in that employee. For many individuals, production levels will drop when dealing with mental health issues. Each year in the United States, over $44 billion is lost in productivity from depression alone, and that's a significant loss to our economy.[3] It's even more substantial on a global scale. According to the National Alliance on Mental Health,

"Depression and anxiety disorders cost the global economy $1 trillion in lost productivity each year,"[4] yet we rarely talk about the tools needed to help these employees who are struggling. Conversations about mental health should be happening in every workplace, opening up the dialogue to the issues millions face in the U.S. and billions face across the globe.

It's not just regular employees. Entrepreneurs tend to be held in high esteem for venturing out on their own, but the risk of starting a business is extremely difficult to handle. Psychology professor Michael Freeman at the University of California San Francisco theorizes that at least one in three successful entrepreneurs suffers from two or more mental illnesses versus about one in five among the general population, according to other studies.[5] Some of our strongest, most successful leaders suffer—once again, I'll state this: *you are not alone.* The time is "now" to address these issues. Attention all business owners: if you fall into this thirty-three percent, my question to you is: "Wouldn't you like to have open discussions about this with your employees?" Talking about these issues will help build trust. My speaking career is the best counselor I could have ever asked for.

Some of the strongest people are feeling the negative effects on their mental health and are taking their lives at increased rates. Our military soldiers, warriors, and leaders are struggling even more than our U.S. civilians. In 2021, research found that 30,177 active-duty personnel and veterans who served in the military after 9/11 have died by suicide—compared to the 7,057 service members killed in combat in those same twenty years. That is, military suicide rates are four times higher than deaths that occurred during military operations. [6] Our country's highly trained, physically and mentally disciplined men and women of the special forces and mainstream military are killing themselves daily due to the ever-increasing issues resulting from the horrors and trauma they have seen while on deployment. The media rarely covers and openly discusses these mental health problems and issues, with the exception of citing statistics. Occasionally their efforts will cause a few ripples in the news cycle, but then the awareness falls away in the quest for higher ratings. Did you know that in 2020, there were 6,146 veteran suicides, which averages 16.8 veterans dying by suicide every day? Additionally, in the two decades between 2001 and 2020, the prevalence of mental health or substance use disorder (SUD) among participants using Veterans Health Administration (VHA) rose from 27.9% to 41.9%.[7] This is depressing and downright sad. These are the men and women who train for years and years to protect our country yet are struggling so badly that ending their life seems like the only way out.

It's heartbreaking to read these statistics. Again, I will repeat—and not for the last time: *you are not alone* in this battle with mental health. Millions are struggling; our strongest men and women are struggling—it's okay to struggle, but it's not okay to not receive help. That is the entire purpose of this chapter. I want to convey that it's healthy to seek help. It's not that big of a deal to have a bad day; we all have them. What really causes emotional distress is the loss of a family member, a rough breakup with a significant other, losing a job or a friend—or any other situation that can affect any of us at some point—mean people and bad grades in school included. We will all face at least one trauma in our lives. When the feelings of sadness and hopelessness continue beyond a two-week period—according to the DSM-5 diagnostic manual used by psychiatrists—that is when people need to seek help.

Close your eyes and take a moment to think about a sporting event, music festival, or being on-the-job with coworkers, and imagine that one out of every five in that classroom, office building, or gigantic stadium could be diagnosed with mental health issues. If you take the pandemic into account and do any basic internet search, you'll find articles and research stating that anywhere from forty to sixty percent of the world struggled with a mental health issue during the global lockdown. I personally think it was even higher than that after talking to hundreds of people during and after the pandemic. The world was struggling; I know I struggled far worse than I could have imagined. When you realize roughly half of the population in the world struggled with something, you realize you are not alone. Here's one of my favorite quotes as of late: "You don't know what you don't know." If you don't know that your ADD/ADHD, bulimia, cutting, depression, social anxiety, or other mental health disabilities are real and need to be dealt with, you just don't know!

No matter what your age, gender, race, religion, or political affiliation is, find help if you are struggling. I beg and I plead with you; if you are struggling with an addiction—a mental health issue—please find help! Don't wait until it's too late like I did. It literally can be the difference between life and death.

CHAPTER 5
ARE YOU OKAY?

Four syllables, three simple words. That's it. It's likely you've asked this question to somebody at some point. Most often, it is rote, without expecting anything back but "I'm fine" or "I'm doing well, thank you." "Are you okay?" is so easy, so powerful, so kind, so gentle—but is often neglected in critical situations when it matters the most. This simple but effective question works. If used in the right moment or situation, it can be a lifesaver. It can also open an emotionally challenging conversation with somebody who is currently struggling with mental health—or more specifically—with suicidal ideations.

"Are you okay?"

Asking a loved one or asking a stranger if they are struggling with thoughts of suicide is scary. It might be the most uncomfortable question you ever ask. The anticipation of what the response might be can be unnerving. If you get the response of, "I'm doing horrible. Honestly, I've been thinking about taking my life," how will you handle that reply? How prepared are you to navigate the wave of emotions? How will you handle yourself during a moment of a potential mental health crisis? If you are like most in our society, you are not trained or ready for it. This is one reason why I'm writing this book, this chapter specifically. I want my readers to know the basics in a crisis situation.

I didn't want to put this section at the end of the chapter or the end of the book in the call-to-action segments. I want this information to be front and center.

There are entire books, courses, curricula, and processes that can be implemented in the aid of somebody who is suicidal. In full disclosure, I'm not a credentialed professional, but I'm often in the middle of the action—where it counts! I'm going to provide you with a brief scenario as one of many options to use in case you haven't had any preparative training. It is better to have some knowledge than no knowledge at all when knee-deep in a conversation with somebody who is suicidal.

ASKING "ARE YOU OKAY?" IN A POTENTIAL CRISIS SITUATION

(Specifically When it Turns to the Topic of Suicide)

You've noticed a coworker, friend, or family member emotionally shut off—they've been acting abnormally over the last few weeks. You finally decided to check on them. It starts with the simple, three-word question, "Are you okay?"

"I'm okay" comes back in response, but since you know there has been a significant change in their demeanor and energy as of late, you ask the question again. "Are you okay?" This second time, you are looking them in the eye with complete concern for their well-being.

They respond with something along the lines of, "I'm struggling, but I'll make it through. It's just been a hard season in my life," as they brush off your attempt to dig deeper. You maintain eye contact and ask the question a third time—with emphasis.

"Honestly, I'm concerned for you. Are you doing okay?"

This time, they open up, stating, "I'm doing really bad. Life feels hopeless." You allow them to vent for as long as they need before you think about responding. After they vocalize their frustrations and pains, you have this feeling that it wasn't enough—you are worried about them. So, you finally ask the hardest question of all questions, "Are you suicidal? Have you thought of taking your life?"

If they say no, you continue the conversation with genuine concern to find out more about what is going on in their life. It might provide insights into the next process of contacting a hotline or finding the right counselor.

If they say yes to the thoughts of suicide, you are now in crisis mode. You ask, "When was the last time you thought of suicide? Do you have a plan to take your life?"

If they have no plan but the thought only briefly occurred to them, stay with them for as long as you can until they feel safe. If they say they had or currently have a plan, *do not—do not* leave their side. Walk with the individual to the school counselor—if on a campus—or the company's on-staff psychologist. *Do not* leave them until they are with professionals. If they have a plan to take their own life, you must stay with them until a professional resource is with them.

Use these resources immediately:

- Call 988 to reach the Suicide and Crisis Lifeline.

- Use your smartphone to text "HOME" to "741741." Volunteers are standing by to text you back.

- Call 911.

When I started this speaking career, I had no idea that I'd hear horrible suicidal stories from those in attendance—and it would happen numerous times thereafter. Right away, I knew I had to be prepared, so I went out and got myself educated! I decided to become a certified Mental Health First Aid instructor from 2019 to 2023. I needed and wanted to know as much information about teen mental health as I could. This increase in knowledge ended up providing me much-needed support to be a more effective and impactful keynote speaker. I don't have all the answers and don't claim to be an expert. What I can do, however, is *open* the *conversation* and provide a few possible options to help in that crisis situation.

THE STIGMA

The stigma of mental health has been deeply ingrained in the news media for years. I've heard comments like, "Depression is not really a thing," followed by, "Shake it off; your life is not that bad. It's only a bad day; things will get better." We all have bad days—people have bad weeks. This aspect of life is normal. Life is not easy. In fact, much of the population has struggled with the global COVID-19 situation over the past few years. As mentioned in the last chapter, one benefit I can see out of this horrible pandemic is the increase in mental health awareness. It has helped combat the mental health stigma. I've spoken to thousands of students, staff, parents, and teachers since the end of the pandemic, and—in my own observations and opinion—I've come to an understanding that now the world in general has a much easier time digesting and loosely understanding mental health issues and topics. Why? The year 2020 ushered in "'rona" fatigue, uncertainties about daily life—and the future, the overall negative outlook on the rules or mandates about infection prevention, the loss of jobs, lives lost, and isolation are just a few of the effects the entire world was facing. An invisible pathogen broke down entire countries and governments, leading to massive shutdowns, a depressed economy, and, for many, the first serious amount of time of isolation in modern times. Mental health problems like anxiety and depression increased as a result.

The COVID-19 virus is mostly considered "endemic" at this point, but the mental health issues haven't magically gone away. Scared to go inside a public space without a mask? Constantly worried about catching this virus? Welcome to the world of an individual struggling with anxiety. Other stressors continue to flourish. Do you spend hours per day comparing yourself to incredibly fit, nearly perfect people on Instagram who have six-pack abs, toned legs, and energy out of this world? After scrolling mindlessly for hours, do you start to feel like a total bum, incapable of ever looking that good? Do you suddenly start to grab layers of excess skin on your hips or thighs, feeling yucky about yourself? Or, while these models of perfection work out at home, you find yourself immobilized, sitting for hours on end watching Netflix, telling yourself to get off the couch and do something. Knowing you need to get up to exercise, you can't summon the energy to do so. Welcome to a similar feeling inside a person suffering from severe depression. No matter how much you tell yourself over and over to get up and start moving, something inside prevents you from getting up from that couch. Deep down, you know you're not lazy. You want to work, you want to get up and experience life, but as soon as you think about moving, every ounce of your energy and excitement to do anything evaporates into thin air. Nothing seems like fun, and the colors in life turn grey, hanging like a black cloud over your head. People don't want to be depressed. People don't want to always feel hopeless. It's extremely difficult to control or manage their moods in a battle with their mental health.

Through awareness and education, we can end the stigma, helping to make resources available to those who feel like this every day. It's aggravating and frustrating to feel lethargic and lack the desire to accomplish the goals you have. You have this urge inside you to get up and conquer life, yet you don't want to do anything. I know—I've been in those shoes countless times. I've had weeks, months, years—nearly a decade—when I was engulfed by an invisible black cloud that seemed to only rain on me. It's hard to be who you want to be when you're surrounded by this life-and-energy-sucking invisible predator—like a vampire feeding off your blood.

Most people diagnosed with a mental health condition can experience relief from their symptoms and live a satisfying life by actively participating in an individualized treatment plan. In one study, they found that nearly seventy percent of the "mental illness in their lifetime met symptomatic recovery, meaning they no longer met the diagnostic criteria for a particular illness."[1] This study shows at least seventy percent of those who struggle can learn to manage and lessen the consequences of their mental health illness if they are willing to ask for help and then "work it" diligently. You have to open up to the conversation and recognize that you are struggling. It takes a tremendous amount of courage and strength to reach out for help. Therapy will work if you give it a chance. It took me about five different counselors until I found the right one who made me feel comfortable enough to believe I could change my thoughts. Keep trying.

SOCIAL MEDIA IS NOT ALWAYS OKAY

Suicides have increasingly plagued schools and the educational system over the last decade and a half. It is the second leading cause of death in teens. A sharp increase in school-age suicides started in the early 2000s, according to the Centers for Disease Control and Prevention, where suicide rates climbed fifty-six percent between 2007 and 2017.[2] Years later, we are discovering a risk factor and trigger for *why* this drastic increase has taken place. In the first five years of this current century, social media outlets like Twitter, MySpace, YouTube, and Facebook became instant-gratification platforms for popularity contests and virtual social hangouts outside of school. They were all created with a positive intent to bring people together using technology. The world was not prepared for the unintended consequences that seem to outweigh the benefits of these popular platforms. And other social media apps such as Instagram, TikTok, YouTube, and more have continued to spring up. These pressures have created havoc on teens' minds and increased anxiety, anorexia, bulimia, peer pressure, suicide, and toxic, unhealthy habits along the way—in addition to being exposed to dangerous predators. According to a study on media usage in the U.S., "In children and teenagers aged between eight and eighteen years, tweens living in households with an annual income of less than 35,000 USD spent 7.32 hours per day on screen media, whereas tweens in households with an annual income of above U.S. $100,000 spent 4.21 hours per day on screen media. Teens living in households with an annual income of less than 35,000 USD spent 9.19 hours per day on screen media, while teens in households with an annual income of above U.S. $100,000 spent 7.16 hours per day."[3] This is baffling. A teen is using their social media apps for 9.19 hours per day—more hours than working a full-time job! This is destroying kids' lives. These data points are relevant because, in Chapter 7, you will see the impact financial insecurity and poverty have on mental health—which social media use and the household poverty rates just mentioned in the study above are directly tied to. Our youth are spending upwards of a third of their life on social media. What would happen if the teens living in low-income households spent their 9.19 hours per day learning about finances or how to start a business? What if they used their phones for education versus scrolling social media? If they dedicated those same hours to bettering themselves, they could help their families break that $35,000 poverty line and decrease the chances of future mental health problems.

IMPORTANT GROUPS TO RECOGNIZE

In every industry and business sector you can think of, mental health struggles exist. Seeds of doubt, embarrassment, fear, and shame seep into every cubicle, office, or top-level executive suite. Many C-suite executives are still hesitant and unwilling to address the current mental health crisis in the room. Many will never admit they themselves, or those close to them, struggle with anxiety, depression, or other mental health conditions. They follow the archaic programming of avoidance, demonstrating an invulnerability that prevents them from being open about mental health. They believe it makes them look or feel weak in front of the hundreds or thousands of their employees who work for them. Their demeanor indicates fearlessness and dominance, in most cases, as they lead their troops into battle. Old-school nonsense.

The world is undergoing a shift where the newest business owners and some older managers have begun to understand the human elements of compassion and love for their employees. The new breed of managers treat employees with respect and care more about their employees' lives than the bottom line. These pioneers are creating a safe environment and opening their doors to individuals who need to talk about their personal lives or struggles. That doesn't mean a quality boss or manager is a certified therapist, but it serves to humanize the employee. Showing somebody that you care about their general well-being can help validate the pain they're in when they need it, and in turn, will boost company morale, leading to increased profit margins and an improved bottom line.

It is critical to communicate that addressing the subject of mental health is no longer off-limits in your small business, corporation, job site, medical facility, school, or university campus. Who knows what personal situations your coworkers are going through? They could have recently lost a loved one or are going through a breakup or a difficult divorce. They could be harboring past traumas and pain deep inside. Even in a healthy and communicative environment, few people like to voluntarily reveal their struggles to others for fear of being uncomfortable and even ostracized. After centuries of mental health stigma, it's going to take time for people to adjust.

Of particular concern in the workplace is the divorce of a couple, which is commonplace in today's world. The sad truth is that over fifty percent of marriages still end in divorce. Most people tend to overlook the anxiety and depression issues divorce can cause. Suicide rates are 2.4 times more likely after a breakup. Men are nine times more likely to take their lives after a divorce, meaning that for every one death by suicide for women, nine men end their own lives.[4] These staggering statistics hit me hard when I was researching data for this book. I was very close to suicide myself with my recent divorce—I had thousands of suicidal thoughts, even had plans on how I would do it after being kicked out of our marital home. Thanks to the Lord above and my precious puppies, I got through it. I have never been so worried I wouldn't make it. It was the darkest moment in my life; darker even than after the accident. As a society, we are not allowed to let these horrible mental health situations impact us in the workplace. It's very difficult to be focused and productive when you feel depressed after experiencing a traumatic event.

PROBLEMS EVERYWHERE, AND IT STARTS EARLY IN LIFE

In 2018, I had four secondary keynote engagements in one week, all in the same town. A trip I will never forget. I had poured my heart and soul into nearly 2,500 lives by week's end. Nearly 250 students emailed, direct-messaged, and texted me—or waited in line for up to an hour to talk to me about their lives. I estimate that about seventy-five percent of the 250 students who reached out or spoke to me referenced substance abuse and mental health issues. It was devastating to hear about their deeply painful and traumatic struggles as young people. It tore my heart into pieces. My ears took in heinous stories from students, some being sexually abused by their siblings or foster parents, many experiencing anxiety and depression so bad that they want to take their lives. A few even pulled up their long-sleeved shirts or hoodies to show the scars from their cutting and suicide attempts. There is always something inside me trying to transfer my power to them while I wait until every student, coach, or employee has had a chance to talk to me. There have been many times I've started to pack up my speaking equipment, ready to head to the hotel to decompress, as a lonely, shy straggler student presents themselves. I'll never forget one kid—scrawny, blond-haired, barely waist-high, and only thirteen years old—who approached me without a greeting or normal pleasantries from a typical student. Before I could say anything, he quietly said, "I've been using methamphetamine on the reg (regularly) for a long time," as if it was no big deal to him (while your jaw drops)—and you're attempting to stay calm, not showing any signs of disbelief for something so horrifying to hear. I attempted to treat this conversation as if it is a normal one to put him at ease. I began to question him about his upbringing. He said nonchalantly that for much of his life he has been in the presence of drugs and danger. His family are addicts, his friends are addicts, and he's surrounded by drugs and criminal activity everywhere he turns. In this situation, what is an impressionable thirteen-year-old to do?

I would like to think hope wins, but hope doesn't fight back too often in this type of situation. As his family goes, he shall go—following suit using meth at the age of thirteen. These moments are some of the most frustrating for me. I can't fault a child for using when their family got them addicted. Being only thirteen, he can't live on his own or move, so he is stuck in this horrible situation he cannot control. This story is one of the millions you can hear in the hallways of every school in the world. The world is messed up, parents and families are messed up, and the vicious cycle will continue into this kid's future— more than likely his life will follow the same path as his family's. My only hope is to be that one spark to ignite their life of avoiding alcohol and drugs and getting help. If I can impact those things, the kid's entire future will be altered. That is my dream every time I speak.

After the week of events concluded, I returned to one of the principal's offices, providing a summary of all the horrible stories I'd heard in confidence. Nonchalantly, the principal admitted she knew about most of these stories, and again, my heart sank. She replied, "Ethan, we have tried to help as many students as we can, *but* we can't do much."

Inquisitively and confused, thinking I could save the world, I asked, "Why?" as if it were a simple fix.

The principal replied, "Ethan, I have these students from the opening bell in the morning until the last bell rings. I do my best to keep them safe and protect them when they are on school grounds, but when they go home, I can't do anything to help them. They go home to their families or guardians and are forced into lives they wish they didn't have." My heart sank some more as I nibbled nervously on my bottom lip. Struggling to find something to say, all I could do was shake my head in disbelief.

Following the discussion with the principal, I furthered my personal investigation and headed to the director of the organization who booked me for all these events. Just as I did with the principal, I provided the director with a short debrief about the week of events. As I dug deeper with questions to the director, the overall situation began to take shape, as I had been asking myself all week, *Why, and what is causing this area to struggle so much?*

The first middle school I spoke at had a very low socioeconomic status, with many of the kids coming from the most impoverished areas within the district—drug use and problems were a normal part of life. Following that tidbit of information, I came to find out that there was only one school counselor for the entire district—a district with almost 6,000 students. Let me repeat that little line: *one* school counselor for the entire district. There was no funding in the district budget to hire any more full-time counselors. In my mind, a much bigger problem was at hand, pushing me to think about a creative solution for this opportunity to serve others. *How are these kids struggling so badly in life before they are even given a chance to be kids?*

Why did all these teens open up to a stranger? They witnessed a bearded, backward hat-wearing, basketball-playing, ex-con, hip-hop-verse-reciting, tattooed-up, grown-ass man with more education than most *open the conversation* and be vulnerable about mental health. It's simple. Me being authentic, honest, real, and vulnerable created a safe vibe to discuss these issues at hand. From my keynote and story, the students realized they were not alone, and I had gone through similar emotional ups and downs as what many were feeling at the time. They understood what they were experiencing and that they were not the only ones in the world feeling that way. They witnessed me describe my own issues in eighth grade, hearing my story about the struggles with peer pressure and the comparison pressure. They heard my story about wanting to be "cool and popular" in middle school, just like every one of them does. They heard my story about the pain I felt when I had a knife to my wrist and wanted to die by suicide in eighth grade. They heard my story on stage in front of everyone, questioning if having that knife to my wrist was just a cry for help or did I really want to die?

These emotional takeaways from my story help *open the conversation* surrounding mental health, peer pressure, and numerous other topics that come from my story. For some reason, my story's strength seems to create a level of vulnerability that empowers audiences to talk about their struggles. Through my struggles on stage, they realize the feelings they have inside and that they are not alone. While sitting in auditorium seats or hard bleachers, audiences start to understand that their personal demons and feelings inside are normal for many. Once audiences feel like they are seen and understood, they become vulnerable and emotionally accessible. Once they open up, they begin admitting to themselves they too are struggling. All they need is a conversation starter—my story is like lighter fluid to their ability to start the conversation.

NOT ONE

From 1993–'94ish and beyond my eighth-grade year, suicide crossed or entered my mind almost every day for ten years of my life. There were only a few years (1998–1999) when I wasn't thinking about dying every day, but 1993–2003 was not an emotionally stable time for me. It wasn't until decades later that I realized why I failed out of the five college basketball programs. Alcohol and drugs were a big part, but I never realized my own mental health issues, which were the underlying root of all my problems. My depression and social anxiety were a huge contributor to why I drank and partied to the point of oblivion. I was masking my mental health by self-medicating to douse the flames of depression and pain inside.

I was an alcoholic, druggie, and partier who enjoyed getting messed up. Nobody during those years of blackouts ever asked why I did what I was doing. They just accepted it. Those around me never knew I was trying to drink myself to death like Nicolas Cage from the movie *Leaving Las Vegas*. I wanted that life of binging on liquor to bring me to an early grave. To speed up the process, I would take drugs hoping I would die. What my friends saw was "E-FISH," the partying hard dude who happened to play basketball but was a bum. People thought I was a basketball loser, which I was. Honestly, I was doing nothing with my life. Failing out of five college basketball programs in five years from 1998–2003 was unheard of. The alcohol and drugs are what everyone thought was preventing me from being successful. The truth was that the underlying factors of darkness, death, and not wanting to live were what was preventing me from achieving my dreams.

Here is a sad fact, one I address now as a speaker. *Not one* of my coaches from those five schools ever asked me what was going on. *Not one!!!!* Not one head coach, not one assistant coach, not one athletic department staff or trainer, *not one* person in administration ever asked what was wrong. *Not one* staff member ever took the time to know me as a person versus the crazy, undersized white point guard who thought he was JWill, Jason Williams, a.k.a. White Chocolate. I cannot stress this enough, but I can't recall ever having a personal conversation with any of my coaches about what was going on. Nobody asked, "Ethan, how's it going? Are you okay?" in the sense of trying to know more about me as a person. They wanted me to perform on the court, perform in the classroom, and play the game so they could keep their job. I'm fully aware that I was not a top recruit in the country. Shit, I wasn't even a top recruit out of high school in my own state. So I was treated like another statistic, another player that can be replaced next year. The coaching world has this engrained philosophy that if a player doesn't fit their system, make grades, and perform, they are replaceable. Why? Because there are hundreds of other players dying to take that spot. Coaches know they can fill any spot as quickly as they need to, as most players are not in the top fifty-to-one hundred players in the country who can and will go on to the NBA. Don't get me wrong, there are a lot of amazing coaches out there in every sport, and they have successful programs, coach the right way, and treat their players and staff like people and not commodities. They have alumni games with players visiting and keep in contact with them throughout the rest of their lives. Those are the coaches that deserve all the credit in the world, an NCAA coach like Roy Williams from a few years back. His players loved him, and he treated them with dignity and respect. They all showed up to his retirement game, just like all of Coach K's players did the following year.

I'll be the first to admit that a lot of the coaches and staff ended up not wanting to deal with my piss-poor attitude. Was I an out-of-control, inflated-ego-driven kid with a bad attitude? Or was I struggling so badly with suicidal ideation and depression because of my mental difficulties that I couldn't care less about anything except for drinking, drugs, and acting out since I hated life and didn't want to be alive? Frankly, the only two reasons I'm still breathing today are because of God and basketball.

One of my workshops, called "Mental Health and Substance Abuse: Promoting Onsite Awareness and Intervention" (Coaches Edition), addresses the signs and symptoms of mental health issues, alcohol use, and substance abuse in their athletes. Yet, it's not just about the athletes, as I flip the discussion and talk about the same topics in the age ranges that coaches are in themselves. The workshop brings awareness to coaches about these tough conversations and how they should interact with their athletes. The end-goal is to have coaches notice those struggling players like I was during my time as a collegiate athlete. By spotting a struggling athlete, coaches now have the ability to help a student-athlete change their life, not just to play ball but for life after sports. Coaches are inundated with work; they must run practices, schedule season games, organize study halls, build community events, and other coaching objectives on top of paying attention to their athletes' mental health. I understand the busyness of coaching; I was an assistant college coach for a few years—coaching is a demanding profession. All the listed objectives above matter, but the greatest asset the coach can have is their players. Knowing your players are doing okay should be the highest priority over scheduling a practice or going over game film with the student-athlete. Protect your assets, and those are your athletes!

It can start with a simple chat in the hallway before practice or a ten-minute life session with each player one time per month. Build a relationship with your players. They are more than job security. Athletes are human beings. Many of them are socially and emotionally fragile, considering that they are away from home, in a new city, and starting a new life not knowing anyone. Being a collegiate athlete is extremely difficult. Many incoming freshmen are first-generation college students. They have nobody to talk to back home who understands the pressures they are facing; a coach can be that sounding board. As a coach, if you help an athlete succeed, they are more than likely going to be willing to tell others you changed or even saved their lives. My high school varsity coach did exactly that. I wouldn't have played at such a high level if it wasn't for Jim Noonan. He didn't put up with any bullshit, and in doing so made me work that much harder to play on varsity during my junior and senior years. I will always be grateful for Noonan and the discipline he forced on to me. His discipline and attention to fundamental details were cornerstones in my playing career.

It wasn't until my sixth college before a coach and I talked about my life. Coach Jeff Culver is currently the head coach at the University of Colorado at Colorado Springs (UCCS) and deserves a huge and substantial amount of credit for my story playing out the way it has. If it wasn't for Coach Culver taking a chance on me, treating me like a decent human being, and listening to my story, I might not be writing this book. I know I wouldn't have had the same academic success at any other schools as I did at the small NAIA Johnson & Wales University (JWU) Denver campus. The JWU campus had perfect class sizes, the best professors I could have asked for, and frankly, I couldn't have imagined a more storybook plot than what happened in my life, again due to Coach Culver. Coach Culver was the first grown man, outside of my family, I ever told about my mental health struggles and suicidal thoughts. He didn't judge me; he treated me like a human being versus some commodity. I'll forever be grateful to him and all the coaching staff at JWU. Coach Moe and Coach Dickins: I love you both and miss those great years together—frankly the best five-year span of my life.

FIGHTING IS SUCCESS

Anxiety is not a weakness, depression is not a weakness, being bullied is not a weakness, cutting is not a weakness, and none of the other disorders that are classified as mental health issues are weaknesses!

Nobody wants cancer, yet hundreds of thousands of individuals are infected with this disease. Are they weak for getting cancer? Hell no—they are strong because they fight it. Cancer patients go through radiation, chemotherapy, blood transfusions, and bone marrow transplants, spending hours in those cold, dark, isolating hospital bedrooms being poked and prodded by doctors—all because they are wicked strong and trying to survive.

Nobody wants heart disease or aneurysms, but people get them all the time. Are these individuals weak for going into the hospital to get checked on? No. If anyone is struggling with these life-destroying diseases, losing the tiresome battle, and passing on into the afterlife, are they weak? Hell mother fucking *no*! The masses would applaud their battle and honor their fight to survive. These warriors kept the Grim Reaper at bay, pushing him out for as long as possible while he continued to knock at the front door. We should have the same public support for the people battling mental health. We should applaud those who break away from its clenches to live another day.

A big reason for this book and why I speak to the younger ages is to get them to address these very issues when they are in middle school, high school, and even college. Why? So they don't become hindered as a thirty-to-forty or fifty-year-old person who neglected their mental health when they were younger. My goal is to stimulate the minds of the youth. I want them to start getting help when they are young, potentially saving them decades of pain and trauma due to the anxiety, fear, and stigma behind their mental health problems. Everyone will face issues; the younger you address and face your mental health, the stronger your foundation will be. My unresolved relationship trauma and sense of being afraid, or not feeling good enough with a long list of my imperfections, were some of the many catalysts that ruined my marriage. My unresolved issues from middle school ultimately came back to destroy the one and only relationship I wanted and needed in this world.

It's easy for me to open up and tell audiences I wish I would have gotten help with my depression in middle school. It's easy to tell them I wish I never drank alcohol and did drugs. What's not easy is addressing my relationship issues during the pandemic versus now when it was all too late. For all the great, amazing things I've done to help others, I lost track of helping myself, neglecting the most important person in my life. Now I'm suffering the consequences and will suffer for the remainder of my life (GGG), however short or long that might end up being.

CALL TO ACTION

Make a list of your friends and close relatives who you can talk with about life. Write out a description of why you can talk to them. Ask yourself these questions:

- Do they listen well?

- Do they allow you to discuss your feelings, issues, or problems?

- Do they make you feel safe and secure?

- Can you tell them intimate details of your life, or is your relationship with them just superficial?

Questions cont.

- Do they immediately have something to say and never allow you to get out your feelings?

- Are they trustworthy or do they tell everyone your business?

Narrow the list down to the top three individuals you can confide in and tell them how much they mean to you; tell them you love them and honor your relationship.

CHAPTER 6

WHAT YOU PUT INTO YOUR BODY MATTERS

If you haven't realized the emphasis I've put on mental health by now, then I'm a poor writer and have much to improve on. I believe mental health is the biggest block to anyone's foundation. The chapters before illustrated that billions of people struggle with the stigmatized issues of mental health. You are not alone in this struggle. Secondly, we discussed how important it is to be vulnerable, allowing for tough conversations about these issues. How can we address them and provide solutions if individuals don't tell others how they think or feel? The next key component to the foundation is physical health—this is not just working out and taking care of your physical fitness. It's not just about weight management; it's much more than that. Without the proper physical health, your mental health will feel the side-effects as well. This includes avoiding many addictive things like alcohol and cigarettes. Physical fitness isn't just about obesity, nutrition, and sleep.

THE MOST DANGEROUS DRUG ON THE PLANET

In most places, alcohol is a societal norm and culturally accepted. It's also big business. Alcohol ads are on every national sporting event; it doesn't matter what sport. These ads are seen at football, basketball, baseball, volleyball games, etc. Alcohol ads are on nearly every TV station, countless podcasts, radio shows, highway signs, and benches where people wait for the bus, sitting with their backs literally touching advertisements that are marketing and promoting a life-altering liquid concoction. My personal opinion: I believe a percentage of the people (especially alcoholics) who can't afford to drive a car, sitting on those public transportation benches covered in alcohol advertisements, will likely spend more on alcohol each month than what the cost would be to own a car in the first place. A heavy drinker consuming fourteen drinks per week at roughly $7 per drink will spend over $5,000 per year, which breaks down to over $400 dollars per month. That is a used car payment and even enough to cover the cost of minimum liability car insurance.[1]

Most of the advertisements we see on TV or in print highlight and show the sexy, fun, young, attractive people living amazing lives while drinking their alcohol brand, hypnotizing the minds of consumers. Advertisements are created to generate a false reality of how much better life is by drinking their products. They influence millions into consuming their alcohol brands, playing with the psychological inse- curities of peer pressure to "fit in," to be "cool," portraying the lifestyle of the actors and actresses in the ads. Sex sells, peer pressure and pop- ularity sell, and people buy products and services to fit in. It's like a magic genie pops up from the bottle once the cork is removed, grant- ing everyone their wish list of friends to join the drinking party. The marketing plans sell the illusion of beautiful friends and great compa- ny every time you drink their alcohol.

The marketing companies don't promote the fact that millions die every year—let me repeat that—millions die every year from alcohol and alcohol-related causes. Alcohol companies and their marketing plans don't talk about this alarming fact because it would be bad for business. I'm not taking anything away from the severe impact that COVID-19 has had on us all in the past two-plus years. In the time between January 2020 and April 5, 2021, over a year and four months, roughly 2.85 million died from COVID in the entire world, and the entire world had gone into a panic. Whereas, by the time a full year rolls around, nearly three million people will die from alcohol and alcohol-related health issues.[2] More *people die* every year from alcohol than the number of people who died from COVID at the height of the global pandemic. At the height of COVID, fewer people died from the virus than those who typically die each year from alcohol. Let that sink in! I'm not trying to take anything away from the scary world of COVID and the millions it's killed so far, but we live in a world that accepts alcohol deaths because people make the choice to drink themselves to death.

Enter an Alcoholics Anonymous (AA) room. Countless stories are told and listened to over free coffee. A handful of the storytellers will likely tell listeners, if asked, that becoming an alcoholic wasn't a choice. Many will say they have a disease that controls their life, as if they have zero choice in the matter of how alcohol impacts the way they think and act. They will claim that alcoholism is a disease that infected them and their lives with poor choices that followed after emptying bottle after bottle of liquor or beer in their drinking days. No matter the sentiment, they will all say alcohol is a dangerous substance, even saying it's the most dangerous drug on the planet—like I say. One of the biggest problems in the United States is over-consuming it. Again, these gigantic companies don't highlight the destruction that their products cause when misused. Alcohol is a depressant to the central nervous system, which slows down the communication process to the brain.[3] Over-consumption of alcohol leads to depression, dependency, and downward spirals, leading to more alcohol consumption.

People see alcohol as a fun social stimulant, often failing to realize the unintended consequences of the excessive drinking that takes place. Excessive drinking causes a $249 billion loss to the U.S. economy every year, and $191 billion of that is caused by binge drinkers. The financial destruction of excessive alcohol impacts our struggling healthcare system at roughly $28 billion, another $25 billion to the criminal justice sector, another $13 billion to car collisions, and the biggest devastation to the economy, $179 billion for loss in workplace productivity.[4] Just imagine the millions of individuals who go to happy hour, drink so much they wake with a hangover, and call into work sick. This causes business owners to lose revenue due to employees drinking themselves out of work, leading to scheduling issues, negative employee relations, and constant hiring and firing of employees who continually miss work due to their excessive drinking habits. Imagine the increase in profit margins companies could retain if they prevented excessive drinking and raised awareness within their organizations. One problem is that many employers promote drinking with happy hours, parties, and events that serve alcohol. They don't think about the DUIs their employees will get after an event or the major loss in productivity at their own company the following day. I'll have more on the impact of alcohol in later chapters.

KILLING STICKS

The 1930s through 1960s—or the "Mad Men" era—was filled with new, creative advertisements of attractive, beautiful, and successful people putting that little white carcinogen-filled nicotine and tar stick into their mouths. At one point, advertisements actually stated that smoking was healthy. Advertising conglomerates controlled the narrative about the products and services they promoted, painting a picture to the world that smoking was a good thing. They helped cigarette companies make hundreds of billions in the process, all while killing millions during that same time frame, not counting the millions of deaths taking place years after battling nicotine addictions. These deaths were not painless either; dying of the various health issues caused by cigarettes was and is exceedingly painful. Horrible deaths resulted from cancer, heart disease, or other serious chronic pulmonary diseases in the lungs, throats, and bodies of these addicted users.

Approximately half a million people die of cigarettes per year just in the United States; that is 1,300 people a day dying from these products. We have laws against commercials promoting cigarettes (passed in 1971) and the FDA has finally banned Juuls (so happy), yet people continue to use and abuse these known killing sticks, even if it kills others around them from second-hand smoke. People don't think about the consequences of their actions outside of how it selfishly impacts them. The point I'm making is that another 41,000 die each year from second-hand smoke. Looking at it from an economic standpoint, smoking cost the United States more than $600 billion in 2018, including nearly $180 billion in loss of productivity due to premature death and exposure to second-hand smoke.[5] It's sickening reading these facts and figures. If all those resources were pooled into stopping food shortages, cleaning the air, and reducing pollution, how amazing would our world be? Yet we want to destroy each other by inhaling death sticks. I could go on and on about this, but this is not my battle. My battle is alcohol, substance abuse, and mental health. But I care about lives—a large percentage of drinkers and drug users use cigarettes. During my drunk nights and drug binges, I would smoke like a chimney. They are commonly tied together. That is why I'm even making a point to discuss it.

SUBSTANCE USE

I tell people all the time that I'm very fortunate to be alive. Frankly, I don't know if I would be alive today if I had access to the drugs that are on the streets today. For a short period of time, I did every pill of ecstasy or mind-numbing, mind-altering pill or line I could get my mouth or nose on. There were many occasions when I had no idea what I was smoking, snorting, or ingesting. If a friend said they had something for me, I would take it, never knowing the quality of the drug or if it was cut with something dangerous. Deep down, I know I took ecstasy that was cut with speed or meth, and regrettably, I don't like to admit that. I remember those highs being substantially different than my normal ecstasy highs. Today, those same drugs I took are often laced with even more potent and dangerous drugs like fentanyl. Again, I'll state that I'm so lucky fentanyl wasn't around when I was growing up. I know I would have tried it or accidentally consumed a drug that had been laced with it. Fentanyl is fifty times stronger than heroin and one hundred times stronger than morphine, and it's a synthetic drug that can be illegally manufactured and distributed easily. The explosion of fentanyl has caused a sharp increase in people who use, and a big part of why over 107,000 died from overdoses in 2021 in the U.S.—with over 290 deaths per day.[6] Many of them were unsuspecting users who had no idea what they were getting at the time of their substance use.

It's not just illegal substances that grabbed a hold of me. I was addicted to any pill I could get my hands on. Every time I went to the doctor and was prescribed a pain medication, I was about to abuse the prescription I was given. I took Vicodin or Percocet like candy when I had access to them. They were the most addictive substance I ever took. I rationalized every time I took one that the doctor prescribed it, and it was okay. When I had access to synthetic prescribed opiates, I would pop three to four pills and drink heavily, chasing the best high I could get out of them. I was fortunate that my prescriptions would run out rather quickly because I would have taken pills every day if I could, like many of the innocent synthetic opioid addicts that we have now. That's how it starts in many prescription pill addicts. They are prescribed an opioid by their doctor for pain, and it grabs a hold of them, leaving them addicted when the person had no such intent. It's sad to think that people get hooked on a doctor-prescribed drug and end up losing their lives down the road. When I go to the doctor, I make sure they don't give me any opioid medication, as I know there is a very high likelihood I'll become addicted. I'd rather be in pain all day than suffer as a pill addict.

IT'S YOUR ONLY BODY

Countless hours are cataloged to study human behavior, collecting data and research to determine what images, ideas, concepts, music, and SEO-specific words will influence the end-users to buy their products. Marketing companies help businesses spend trillions of dollars influencing buying decisions. It's a near-perfect science. A large portion of these companies dominate the advertising and marketing platforms so they can generate astronomical sales and provide a consistent product. One of the biggest issues and problems: a good percentage of the products are not healthy for the body and our brain.

Today's data, research, and science can prove that if we decide to take care of our bodies, we can live longer and healthier. But the reality is, we can die at any given moment due to an accident or our body deciding to fail us, no matter the healthy choices you make in life. Deciding to take care of your body will put your life and potential longevity into your own hands based on the decisions you make. There is a direct correlation between a person's physical health, mental health, and their overall well-being.

The human body is fantastic at recovering, replacing virtually trillions of cells every few years. New research says our bodies replace around 330 billion cells per day.[7] This is not me making up some random fact to make my book flow better or to psyche myself into thinking "I'm staying young." If you take care of your body, it will last a long time. Our bodies are much like an automobile. If you take care of a vehicle, stay up-to-date on your oil changes and air filters, drive safely, and avoid potholes or off-roading, chances are the car will last a very long time. If a part begins to fail, you can replace it and keep the car moving along, barring any surprise component failures.

One of my favorite players of all-time, and current favorite NBA star, invests heavily in his body. It's been rumored he spends upwards of $2 million per year taking care of his body and his mental health, allowing him to play at an elite level, heading into his twenty-first season at thirty-nine years old. Lebron James is ranked anywhere between the top one through the top five greatest players in NBA history. Arguably the greatest NFL quarterback to ever put on an NFL jersey, Tom Brady, has his own training philosophy. It has garnered some negativity from some in the fitness world, yet it visibly worked for him during twenty-three years as an NFL MVP quarterback. Working on making his muscles elongated and flexible, mixed with a healthy diet and enough water to quench an elephant, his personal workout philosophy allowed him a very long NFL career well into his mid-forties, while using meditation and visualization as tools to prepare for the grueling life of an NFL superstar.

LeBron James and Tom Brady will both go down as two of the greatest in their respective sports. They've invested heavily into their mental toughness and their bodies, which is why they are in my discussion about being GOATs. They bet on themselves and proved all the doubters and haters wrong. During this process of belief, they were ahead of their times, knowingly and willingly driven to invest in their bodies. In doing so, they've not only had great lives but abnormally long professional careers. Why? Because they both took care of their physical and mental health. They became two of the most dominating sports figures in history. They fit one of the themes within this book: people who succeed bet on and believe in themselves—something anyone can do. Believe in yourself. Nobody will do it for you!

CALL TO ACTION

Do something. Anything!

Start today on improving your life by just one percent. That's all! Improve the most important part of your life, your foundation. Start with one brick at a time. Add another brick tomorrow until you have built up a solid foundation for the new-and-improved you.

GET YOUR ASS ACTIVE

Here are a few small, meaningful examples of changes that can add up to making big improvements to your foundation.

- **Week 1**: Walk around the block for a week. Substitute one day of sodas with one day of water.

- **Week 2**: Add in a fifteen-minute jog around the block two days a week and keep walking the other days. Substitute two days of sodas for two days of water.

- **Week 3**: Increase your jog to twenty minutes around the block and add fifteen push-ups before or after the jog. Substitute three days of sodas with three days of water.

- **Week 4**: Stay with the twenty-minute jog around the block and fifteen push-ups, but now add another small brick to your foundation. Add fifteen sit-ups and fifteen jumping jacks to your thirty-minute routine. Continue building on week three with the same substitution of three days of sodas and three days of just water, then add reading ten pages of a book (or equivalent) or meditate for five minutes to improve your mind. Slowly add and build your foundation with more objectives to each week.

Remember, these are just suggestions, and you can add or subtract anything you want. The purpose is to add slowly and build the healthy foundation for you to live on.

CHAPTER 7

BEING BROKE IS MORE THAN BEING BROKE

"The rich rule over the poor, and the borrower is slave to the lender."
– THE BIBLE, PROVERBS 22:7

Just as this chapter title says, being broke sucks. Being broke is far more than just having it rough financially. Financial instability and being financially destitute are common risk factors and struggles in the mental health realm. A Wang study revealed that "Stressful life events (SLEs) also directly impact the rate of suicide. Individuals who experience significant losses to their financial, emotional, or physical health, or are subjected to violence or abuse may also be predisposed to suicide." The entire world just experienced SLEs due to the global pandemic. Wang's research studied 34,000 individuals within a one-year period and found that "Financial stressors had the largest impact on attempted suicides, followed closely by violent assault. Specifically, financial problems led to more suicide attempts than nearly all of the psychological conditions, except depression."[1]

It's as simple as this—being broke can lead to an increased chance of suicide. Life is significantly more difficult when having financial issues. This can and will lead to a rocky foundation. Money can't buy happiness, but it can take away significant issues that impact and affect one's mind and psyche. Being financially poor prevents things like education and limits access to appropriate medical help in times of need. Divorce can destroy the financial stability of a partnership, causing one to lose everything they worked for together.

Scare tactics worked well for the financial industry until roughly the year 2020. The general public has been misled to believe that the finance world is an intimidating place. I operated under these scare tactics until I did something about it by educating myself and earning a minor in finance. My world of understanding about the financial markets, global economy, and money changed drastically. As mentioned above, my mindset about money was like millions of others. I thought that only the best and brightest minds from Ivy League universities could fully understand the financial markets and how to invest dollars, preventing the average person from pursuing any knowledge of how to invest and the power of compounding interest. I believe that all changed when the boom of Financial Technology (FinTech) became popular with the public.

In today's world, nearly anyone with a cellphone and internet capabilities can have numerous investing platforms for everyday people at their fingertips to build their portfolios and learn how to invest. Robin Hood, a new popular financial trading platform aimed at the new generation of investors, has allowed common folks to trade stocks or other financial products for the first time. People would see the new cycles and media and think, "I can't invest; it's too complicated. There are very smart professionals who will take advantage of me," and self--talk themselves out of even pursuing more knowledge. There is a significant misconception that investing in stocks, bonds, index funds, and any other type of investment vehicle is too difficult to grasp. Yes, it can become very complex the more you try to learn, but the basics of investment for anyone are simple.

Anyone—I mean anyone—can be better prepared to manage their money, even if they are making minimum wage. That doesn't mean making millions of dollars day trading is for everyone—it takes incredible skill and discipline that very few have. All it means is setting up a simple recurring deposit (investment) from a bank account that can go directly into an index fund, which takes very little effort to start slowly and consistently building a foundation of a better financial future.

It's hard if you are living paycheck to paycheck and need every cent of every dollar just to get by. Even when you are eating ramen noodles, are in debt with college loans, or are struggling to have enough money for a cell phone bill, you can still put money away for the future. If you can manage to cut out one less thing to spend money on, you can begin to see progress. Anybody who buys alcohol or smokes cigarettes has no excuse not to invest—if they make a choice to prepare for the future versus spending their limited funds on alcohol or cigarettes. If you invested what the average price of a pack of cigarettes costs each month, or that $5,000 dollars I mentioned in the previous chapter about what an alcoholic spends per year, the starting investor can begin to build for the future. For example: Take that average of $400 per month an alcoholic spends and automatically deposit it into an index fund and continue to take public transportation. With the most basic example I can provide, if a thirty-year-old individual invests that $400 into an index fund every month until they hit retirement at sixty-five years of age, they will have a nice nest egg, depending on the rate of return. If they average a low five percent return, which is below the historical average of the stock market, that $400 dollars per month, after thirty-five years of compounding interest, would become roughly $450,000. Not a bad return for taking public transportation and remaining sober.

A basic understanding of the market and learning to invest when you're young is so important. It wasn't until my early thirties that I knew the concept of "compounding interest." I believe a finance class or course should be mandatory for every student to take, more so than the ancient history classes, geology, or anthropology classes I dreaded going to. Did I have a financial class in middle school or high school? Not that I'm aware of. Was it a potential elective I could have taken? I have no idea—I was never told about it. But the point is, it should be *mandatory*, like reading and writing. When students become adults and don't have any basic understanding of banks, checking accounts, savings accounts, credit card debt, or other debt, they are stuck. Which in turn could leave them with mental health issues and problems like anxiety and depression, creating rough marriages, stress in family life, and a constant feeling of being in quicksand. Poverty is emotionally draining and exhausting.

It's likely that most individuals will receive their financial education from their parents. That is where I received the early bulk of my financial education growing up. My parents worked very hard to change our family's financial outcomes. They went from broke, living in a trailer, to well off and have done incredibly well for themselves. Yet, they know basically zero about financial planning and helping make their kids financially literate; good luck with that! They gave a dumb, uneducated junior in high school a credit card and said, "Use it sparingly." That didn't last very long, as I maxed out the card multiple times just on shoes and clothes in the first few months—then they took it from me. When I got my first checking account, my parents said, "Make sure you balance your checkbook." Did they show me how? No. Did anyone in school show me how? No. That was the extent of my financial literacy education entering into my freshman year in college. I was so prepared for the real world (with the biggest amount of sarcasm I can muster). I don't blame my parents. They weren't educated about money when they were growing up. How were they going to educate and train me or my siblings? They were not prepared, and it impacted the first ten-plus years of my adult life.

In this book, I have mentioned many regrets in my life. I wish I could have a do-over. This is one of them. I wish I could go back to the age of eighteen and implement what I learned from my finance degree at thirty years of age. I'd be a heck of a lot closer to being retired by now just by investing a few hundred bucks per month in my early adult years, but now I'm chasing retirement like most people in my age demographic.

All parents face difficult times raising kids—even the simple things are hard, like teaching them not to run out into the street, protecting them from eating Tide Pods, teaching them to buckle their seatbelts, and the infinite number of other life-altering choices kids make each day. If the parents lack a financial education, barely making ends meet, living paycheck to paycheck, how will they educate their kids in financial literacy? They won't! The lack of financial education is why generations of families will continue to remain poor, and it's not because they don't work, don't try, or want to be broke. They lack the education. Don't get me wrong; it takes work, consistency, dedication, and a plan to invest. It's hard, especially at a young age when you are barely making enough to keep the lights on. It is up to the person to choose how they want to plan for their future. Anyone can invest using the incredible technology we all have access to on our phones, tablets, and laptops. It comes down to the choices they want to make. Do I invest these hundred dollars, or do I go out and try to impress people who don't give two shits about me and buy those $100 headphones? The choices add up.

LACK OF COMPOUNDING EDUCATION

Even as a little kid, I always enjoyed learning. Let me preface this by saying I enjoyed learning things that were important to me, never caring about some irrelevant jeopardy history question that I would have to regurgitate for some quiz and never need again. This sentiment was evenly applied to every boring class from Brit-lit, chemistry, and math to any other class I took in high school that I don't remember. All of which I would basically take zero away from. If you need an image or a poster boy for the face of an immature, developmentally delayed, late-starting individual, look no further than the back of this book for my author picture.

Research often states that females' brains typically mature years earlier than us childish men (me included—again, I'm a poster boy of delayed development). A woman's brain is fully developed as early as the late teens and early twenties. As for us straggling men, we are on a delayed maturity path that usually begins to function in our mid-twenties, upwards of twenty-five and twenty-six years of age. Just like everything I do, I was pushing the boundaries with my late development, causing higher data set numbers. It wasn't until the age of twenty-four that life began to click and make sense, and twenty-eight years of age before I began acting like an adult.

It took me sitting in twenty-three-hour isolation in a prison cell to switch the light on. Not the best place in the world to realize that I was in control of my life and in control of the choices I was making. It took being surrounded by constant negativity, wearing prison boots, and the same three sets of green pants and three sets of green, V-neck t-shirts, along with a set of five white undershirts, all of which were rotated for the days of the week, to snap me into maturity. My low-performing brain finally caught up to my actual age in those brightly lit cells.

Prison was intended to stall my education, and it does that for most of the inmates incarcerated within those cells, but boredom, isolation, and time piqued my interest into deep learning. I started to realize that I needed knowledge and, more importantly, an education to change my life upon release. Without an education, I was on the path to working a dead-end job the rest of my life because I was a felon.

Fast forward about four years after my release to when I was attending my sixth college for basketball while on ISP (intensive supervised parole) inmate status. This happened to be the tenth out of eleven total colleges that I had been enrolled in up to that point. Johnson & Wales University was the first project-based university I had ever attended. It was the first time in my life and path of education that I thrived in the classroom. My love for school was ignited. I enjoyed school and knew what I wanted to do in life—it was amazing. My time at Johnson & Wales University was the best five-year span of my life. The rush and thrill were so enjoyable that I didn't just finish with one bachelor's degree, I needed more. I tell audiences I got greedy with degrees, and after the completion of my first bachelor's degree, I decided to get a second one along with three minor degrees. All in one academic year for the hell of it. It wasn't until my second bachelor's degree and my second minor that I was introduced to a financial literacy course. Yep, that's right. I was thirty years old and working on a second bachelor's degree and a second minor degree before I knew anything about the stock markets, the concept of compounding interest, and the plethora of other incredible and life-changing information that is crucial for individuals to succeed financially.

Question. Where was this life-changing education in middle school and high school when it should have been mandatory? Like I said earlier, I didn't receive any of it. Not one time did I have a class that discussed or focused on financial management, starting a business, planning for retirement, or how to invest in stocks, let alone one that taught about the financial ruin and destruction that credit cards, high-interest loans, and college debt could do to one's life. At the age of thirty, I was so far behind the eight ball when it came to financial preparedness due to the broken public school system that taught me nothing I needed to survive in the real world. It's complete BS!!! It's no wonder we have poverty issues when banks and public loan sharks have a stranglehold on the financially uneducated.

"Everyone you meet in life is fighting a battle you know nothing about."
– UNKNOWN

Most people living in poverty will remain broke, poor, struggling from paycheck to paycheck, not because of a complex financial environment, but because of the lack of education. Not only is being poor often a lifelong and generational struggle, but financial destitution is also one of the most difficult, ongoing issues that can destroy a person's mental health. And that is why a financial education is so important to me. Those who struggle with mental health often struggle financially, and those who struggle financially end up struggling with mental health. What comes first, the chicken or the egg? Both are influenced by one another.

Here is some food for thought: half of adults in problem debt —debt that becomes unmanageable, with the individual struggling to pay just the minimums—also have a mental health problem. People with problem debt are twice as likely to develop major depression as those not in financial difficulty. People in problem debt are twice as likely to think about suicide as those not in financial difficulty, even after controlling for other factors. Debt and financial burdens are significant risk factors and triggers for somebody's mental health. When you're poor and finances are non-existent, your foundation faces a gigantic crack in it. People with debt are three times more likely to have a mental health issue, especially depression, anxiety, and psychotic disorders. Financial stress is the second-most common cause of suicide, after depression.[2] Let me repeat that data: financial stress is the second most common cause of suicide. Let me further this discussion and emphasize the amount of research and data backing these potential life-ending issues around finance. According to the "Silent Killer Report" from England, over "420,000 people in problem debt consider taking their own life in England each year, and more than 100,000 people in debt attempt suicide. These same individuals in problem debt are three times more likely to have considered suicide than people who are not in problem debt. Long-term factors such as persistent poverty and financial insecurity can put people at risk of becoming suicidal, as can sudden triggers like the intimidating and threatening letters people receive from lenders."[3] Research shows money stress can make people up to twenty times more likely to make a suicide attempt.[4] Being broke doesn't just suck, it drastically and significantly increases the likelihood of mental health problems and suicide. In the next part of the chapter, I'll show you how much it impacted my life when I was on the brink of suicide due to financial instability.

BEING BROKE NEARLY KILLED ME

If I had known that my speaking career would involve living the life-style of a starving artist or a struggling "van down by the river" motivational speaker like Chris Farley from the great Saturday Night Live skit, I would have quit a long time ago. This career has left me with my back against the wall numerous times, broke and financially destitute. Again, I would have never started down this speaking path if I knew what I know now. I would have stayed in coaching basketball or found a privately operated fiduciary company that graciously overlooked and allowed felons into the workforce. I would have diligently worked my way up the corporate ladder to make real money and become a c-suite type leader in the industry. My newfound joy and knowledge of the finance world blinded me after taking those finance courses. I was consumed with the stock market and found a career path I wanted to pursue. Yet my ambition was blinded by my past. I was completely unaware, at the time of earning my finance minor, that publicly traded financial companies would not hire me due to a rule by the SEC that prohibited the hiring of felons. If I would have known this simple fact, I wouldn't have taken the three job interviews at large public financial firms that basically shunned or laughed in my face after my openness about my felony in the interviews. I even had a phone interview where the hiring manager hung up on me in the middle of the job interview. After experiencing all the doors slamming in my face, a mentor and friend, Marcel, thought it was time to find a new path, saying, "Stop beating your head against the wall and focus on just one new career," alluding to leaving the finance world altogether. That influence led me to pursue this speaking career.

If I would have known how incredibly difficult starting a speaking career would be financially, I would have never chosen it and gone into one of the other possible career paths. Outsiders have no clue how difficult it is to be a full-time speaker and make a living at it. The reality is, only a small percentage of speakers make consistent, great money. It's a dog-eat-dog world when every speaker in the world, more than likely, thinks they should be speaking at every event—the competition is fierce.

Being broke sucks, but then on top of that, because of the adulation I receive from being onstage, it seems to make the mental health stressors even harder to manage in my real life. Being broke after receiving all this adoration has left me curled up in the fetal position a handful of times in 2017, 2021, and 2022.

In January 2017, I was flat broke with nothing but maxed-out credit cards, no paid speeches, and no money coming in for nearly four months due to a lying booking agent. The agent kept telling me that I had a handful of events booked under his management and events were lined up on the speaking schedule. Not questioning his word, I believed him and was dependent on these bookings to survive. Slowly, each week's events kept getting canceled or pushed into the future. Finally, I took things into my own hands (a little later than I should have) and started calling the schools that he had said were booked. Each school and athletic director I called would say, "I've never heard of you [being me as a speaker], and we have never spoken to this person [agent] you are referring me to." I ended up confronting this agent, yet he kept lying about every event that he had booked. I started contacting other keynote speakers he represented and found out he was doing similar things to them, even taking events from his speakers. Let's just say I pulled the right strings, and the other speakers, who were much higher-priced speakers than I, began taking him down—eventually destroying his lying agency. It was a pleasure watching him fall, yet that joy didn't help me at all, and I was still on the brink of collapse financially as a speaker.

Warning: the following contains a detailed description of suicidal ideation. Please skip to page xx if you would not like to read it.

There was a point where I was in my bedroom with the shades down, glancing over and over at my bathroom door. For two weeks in January 2017, all I could visualize was going into my shower and slitting my wrists with the old, rusty razor that had been standing at attention for months on end in the shower basket. It was like watching a horror movie over and over, watching the scene play out in my head as if I had a view from above. It was so vivid, I could see myself walking into the shower, turning on my Bose speaker as loud as I could, proceeding to close the dingy glass sliding doors on my shower, turning on the hot water, glancing up at the sky, and saying goodbye. Grabbing the razor, I would grip its handle tightly, directly aiming the blade straight down on my wrist so the blood would drain faster, flowing down my palms, all to be rinsed away by the shower water as hot steam filled the air. I watched the blood pour into the drain, leaning my back against the shower wall, slowly sliding down to a sitting position with my head between my knees, watching the pool of blood grow wider and wider as I died right then and there.

Then visions of my brother, and roommate of nearly ten years, came into focus as I envisioned him heading directly to his basement room after coming home from work like any other day. This is how it visually played out in my mind. He would hear my music playing full blast and the shower running, thinking nothing was out of the ordinary. He'd turn on his PlayStation and put on headphones, about to buckle down for a few hours to play video games like he always does after work. My brother would be dressed in some nasty, classic sweatpants—a Christmas present our mom bought him many years earlier—and an equally disgusting, yellowed white t-shirt. A couple of hours would go by before he realized that something is very wrong. The laundry room is filling with cold water that is pouring down the ceiling from my shower on the second floor! His six-foot-seven frame would leap up the stairs, pushing my bedroom door open while he lunged at the bathroom door. The steam would be gone, as the hot water heater would have gone cold. He would whip open the sliding glass doors and find my lifeless body lying in a heap in the corner of the shower stall.

✵

The vision quickly disappears. Tears pour down my face as I'm still lying in the fetal position on my bed in my dark room. Slowly, I sit up and shake my head as if to say, "What the fuck?" I tell myself over and over, *I can't do that to my brother. I can't ruin the rest of his life. He would never forgive himself.* Wiping the last of my tears, I gather myself and open the bedroom door, slowly meandering to the kitchen, acting like nothing horrific had just played out in my severely depressed, suicidal mind. I can't kill myself. I have nowhere to turn, nowhere to go. Other than my family, there is not one person I trust in this world to ask for help right now. I'm not going to my parents—they are struggling too. They don't have any extra money to help me. Besides, I have too much pride to go back for help. They've already done countless things to help me when I've failed. I'm not going back to them. Two names pop into my head. The first, I can't go to. The second…

The early morning light shined down on our table outside the little coffee shop, looking over the serene scene of downtown Denver. An older gentleman who vaguely reminds me of my father, a mentor and friend—doesn't realize he is about to become a lifesaver. Little did he know that the morning we met at the coffee shop was my last resort. Bemo had no idea that in the last few days preceding this coffee meeting, I had been picturing and embracing the idea of leaving this world and giving up. On the brink of losing everything. The friendly pleasantries passed, and he asked, "Fish, what's going on? Why did you ask me here?" I took a deep breath and began to vent. Sentences of anger from a speaking agent that left me in financial ruin, frustration about life coming out in salty tears pouring from my eyes. I explained the situation to him, the lying, the calls to schools, specific contacts, and hearing "We have never heard of you, and we never talked to him," referring to the booking agent. All the phone calls I made to the schools confirmed the agent was lying, cheating, and misrepresenting my future events. That agent left me penniless with no possible events until mid-February, which I had already booked on my own. I had no other options but to come to Bemo for help. Bemo looked in amazement but kept cool and calm. This dude has always been a man with the ability to keep a smile on and believe that life is great. His philosophy in this world is "bad things happen; it's how you address them that matter." So no matter the trying times he faces, a smile is on his face. If I could only bottle up what Bemo has for dealing with the world and sell it, I'd be a rich man and wouldn't have these financial burdens.

Sucking up my pride and embarrassment—as the only people I've ever borrowed money from were my dad and brother—humbly and broken, I asked, "Bemo, can I borrow some money? I'll pay you back next month. I have events booked. I'll give you loan shark numbers," referring to a high-interest loan I would pay back.

His hesitant reply, alluding to the potential of our friendship being lost over money: "Fish, I wouldn't charge you anything. Are you sure about this?"

"I won't let you down; you mean too much to me. Besides, I have nobody else to ask." I can only imagine the hesitancy in his decision as he more than likely played out numerous situations where he loaned money to others, never getting it back and losing those friendships along the way. He said, "Let me think about it," and a few hours later, he texted me saying, "Fish, let's meet at the same spot around 7 a.m." The following morning, at the same coffee shop, he handed me a check, never fully understanding or knowing the full extent of what he had done for me. He didn't know I was suicidal; he didn't know that I visualized how I was going to end my life. All he knew was I was struggling financially because of this speaking career and this agent who fucked me. That day was far more than money; it was trust and brotherly love. He more than likely saved my life that day.

For hours and hours the week before, I laid in my bed thinking about dying and how I couldn't live like this anymore. The embarrassment, shame, and pain that I could survive the accident, take a man's life, survive prison, parole, school, and college basketball as an inmate, yet I couldn't create and sustain a business and career to pay my own mortgage was beyond my comprehension. To top it off, just a few days before asking Bemo for a loan, I'd received a phone call from a student who had seen my speech and watched me grow over the years as a speaker. He said, "Ethan, you are the most successful person I have ever met. Can I interview you for my project in school?" This nearly broke me. The student had no idea that I was on the brink of suicide only hours prior to his call. His call nearly ended me. My stomach dropped to the floor in disappointment, embarrassment, and shame. He unintentionally made me feel worse than I already had because I felt like a fraud. My negative thoughts went directly to my plans for ending it. Over and over, this scenario played in my head. I couldn't take being a failure anymore. *I've let everyone down, and I don't deserve to be alive. Because of me, a man (Bill) had died in vain in that horrible car accident.* Worse, I'd let God down. It was time to give up. I had no fight in me left. Then Bemo came to the rescue and aided me at a low point of my life.

This speaking career has been a continuous uphill battle. The financial burdens of being a speaker have yet to level out over the years. Like I said in the beginning of the chapter, if I knew I would be struggling this long and hard financially, I would have never chosen this career. But now I'm forty-three years old, "pot committed" (a poker gambling term), and have very few options otherwise to succeed. I've poured everything into this career, every ounce of energy, every penny and resource I've had access to, and the light at the end of the tunnel is coming. I can feel it.

CALL TO ACTION

FINANCIAL PLANNING

Disclaimer: I'm not a certified financial planner. I do have a basic college minor in finance and just recently passed the Texas State Insurance

Licensing Exam, but I have no after-university financial certifications. I have a decent understanding of financial instruments but lack all advisor credentials. There are thousands of qualified authors, speakers, trainings, and programs to learn from. I'm not here to give financial advice, just to show some simple ways to lessen the negative impact financial problems can have on an individual's mental health.

Here are some simple and effective methods to begin planning for a better financial brick in your foundation.

- Set a budget—know exactly what comes in and what goes out of your bank account.

- Avoid credit cards/high-interest personal loans—they will keep you broke—use for emergencies and do not purchase material things or vacations. If you do use the cards, pay them off every month before the interest begins to take hold of the account.

- Begin investing five to ten percent of your paychecks into an index fund—set up an automatic withdrawal from your paychecks each month. As they say, "Set it and forget it."

You can do one of these, two, or all of these options to better prepare yourself for the future. The key is to start, no matter how small or little you contribute—*do it*.

PART 2

WITHOUT STRUGGLE, THERE IS NO GROWTH

Approximately eight billion people live on God's green earth. The vast majority of the eight billion have faced some form or type of struggle. The destitute, the poor, the middle class, millionaires, trust fund families, and even the billionaires with ungodly amounts of money experience struggle at some point in their lives. Two of the world's richest couples went through divorces in the past few years: Jeff Bezos and Bill Gates. Even the wealthiest face traumatic events and struggles. The rich might face completely different struggles than the rest of the world, but they face struggles nonetheless. The point is, everyone will face struggles based on everyone's situation. Learning from the struggles you face is what will make you grow and become resilient.

Part 2 addresses the variety of struggles I've faced. Many of them were due to underlying factors such as social anxiety, negative self-talk, outside influences, and the ignorant thought process of "it can't happen to me." Being unaware of the underlying factors of my struggles shifted my mindset, sending me into a downward spiral of depression, suicidal thoughts, addictions, fear, and lack of focus, resulting in hitting a massive rock bottom. Today, I consciously choose to make my past struggles into present-day strengths by focusing on an overall positive future. I've learned to adapt, turning a horrible situation into an amazing career helping others. Today, I'm living with purposeful intent because I've turned my struggles into growth. You can do the same.

CHAPTER 8
TITO THE ANXIETY MOSQUITO

Hands sweaty, heart pumping; it's not adrenaline, it's anxiety. "I get it. I'm the worst. But so are you," Tito speaks out nervously as Nick responds, "I know. Andrew hates me."

Tito reaffirms Nick's fears by saying, "So does Seth. They are probably making fun of you right now."

Quickly, the anxiety level skyrockets inside Nick, causing new strata of anxiety and fear that Nick has never experienced before. New layers of negativity begin consuming Nick's thoughts, taking over Nick's mind. Tito isn't finished. As a matter of fact, Tito is far from done.

Moments later, Tito starts spewing anxious and negative thoughts like raindrops in an April shower, causing a new path of self-rejection and self-loathing in Nick's young mind. "You're going to have the worst summer. Everyone is going to hate you. They are going to know you are a selfish prick." All this chaos in Nick's thoughts sends him into a full-on freakout. The next few minutes illustrate a full-on panic attack. Nick is surrounded by hundreds of Titos speaking anxious and disturbing thoughts into his young, preadolescent mind, leaving Nick exhausted and deflated as a person.

The adult animation, *Big Mouth*, on Netflix, episode "Introducing Tito the Anxiety Mosquito—Big Mouth"[1] is about a group of teen friends facing puberty. The spin, their inner dialogue and inner voices are played by a wide variety of hormone monsters. The show is filled with raunchy adult content, but that is to be expected from the actors and producers from Nick Kroll and The League. In my unprofessional critique of shows, I personally think it's a fantastic work of art. It conveys the inner battles many teens face during puberty. These characters all have underlying stories tied to the mentality many teens face in today's world. It takes a comedic, overly embellished look inside the minds of teens, and I think it does a great job of highlighting the issues teens face. I say this knowing my thoughts were like many of the situations the characters faced when I was in middle school and high school.

Life is hard as a teen. Teens have so much to deal with. Their bodies are undertaking massive changes emotionally, socially, and physically. Let's not forget the family or guardian relationships that tend to become icy in most cases of teens and parents. Some teens are blatantly laughed at and made fun of for wearing the wrong clothes or having the wrong set of friends. Kids are afraid to ask questions in class for fear of being made fun of or judged. If a student is perceived to ask a "dumb" question in elementary school, it can change the entire direction of their life. It can prevent the student from ever wanting to ask a question again for fear of being seen as stupid by their classmates. I never asked questions in school because I was afraid of being picked on. The popular kids began making fun of the student who asked a question, ostracizing them from learning how to make new friends and important connections that ultimately increase the potential of future mental health issues, destroying any ability to socialize and learning how to deal with other people. They, in turn, internalize their pain, retreat, and become a shell of themselves and who they were supposed to be in their adult lives, all because of raising their hand in class. A large portion of people brush this off, saying it's a part of growing up, and it is. Yet these single moments in a student's education will change who they are to the core, molding insecurities into who they become.

Over time, the youth will begin to create anxieties, negative self-talk, and inner dialogue that can lead to insurmountable and challenging fears as adults.

Ask Google or Siri to find research on the number of thoughts a typical person has each day. Depending on the multiple articles or research papers that magically appear based on the algorithm of one of these giant search engines, most of the searches will find articles stating the average person has somewhere between 35,000 and 65,000 thoughts every day. Your age, maturity, life experience, nature or nurture philosophy, religion, and countless other defining terms all play into the sheer volume of 35,000 to 65,000 thoughts going through somebody's mind. I have a difficult time trying to conceptualize just how many thoughts that is—it doesn't make sense. It's even harder to imagine when a bunch of Titos are flying around inside the mind constantly spewing venomous poisons of self-loathing and doubt.

MY CHILDHOOD TITOS

Life was easy until the early weeks of seventh grade. I felt like a regular kid going about my daily life in school. I tended to focus on recess and lunch far more than any topic taught by my teachers, caring less about class than the sports I would play during recess. Something shifted when I hit those middle school doors. My adolescent mind began having thoughts like Tito, Nick's anxiety mosquito, from the opening of this chapter. It was like two atoms shot at each other at the speed of light, and kaboom, my barely functioning frontal lobe, with its few thousand thoughts per day, began having upwards of 65,000 thoughts. Almost instantly, I was no longer concerned with just sports; now girls, popularity, and appearance began consuming my thoughts. Thoughts began spinning uncontrollably, whispering, *Will I sound dumb? Is it the right thing to say? Will they laugh at me? Does she think I'm ugly? Do they think I'm crazy? Can they hear my thoughts? Oh, fuck, they can hear me thinking about them. Shut your mind off. Walk away.* This internal dialogue took place within the first few moments in the hallways during our ten-minute, between-class breaks. I dreaded these moments, and the worst part was this moment happened at least seven different times per day over the next six years of my middle school and high school life.

Groups of other students in the hallways made me anxious; I felt uncomfortable socializing in the hallways. Between classroom breaks, I'd go straight to the gym to play a game of "21." It's a type of basketball game where individuals try to score twenty-one points versus all other players in the game. The game is great for developing offensive skills and defensive rebounding. It was the only place I felt comfortable.

Most days, the gym was open, but on the days that it was closed, my head would lower, avoiding eye contact with as many other students as possible. I found it easy to navigate through the hallways when I didn't make eye contact with others. Most days I was unable to turn off the internal berating going on incessantly in my head. *What's going to happen? My life is over. I can't do this. Man, I'm a pussy. I'm a little bitch. I'm nothing*, never realizing all this negative thinking, negative self-talk and self-doubt would layer on itself for years and years to come. I was oblivious to the fact that I was writing my conscious and unconscious programming for how I would operate in social situations. Those thoughts at the ages of twelve and thirteen contributed heavily to the fears I still have to this day, especially in any public situation. I wish I could go back and reprogram my thinking, but I can't.

The onset of puberty laughed at me like a cruel jester. Puberty avoided me in seventh grade. I was one of the last boys in my grade with smooth, hairless armpits and not one random facial hair on my face. This delayed process would alter how I felt about myself. My sister says she caught me using a marker to draw black lines, aka fake armpit hair, underneath my arms. I don't recall that happening, but I probably buried that humiliating moment of being caught by my sibling drawing in armpit hair deep in the recess of my memory.

With little-to-no testosterone coursing through my veins, my delayed puberty glands intentionally left me socially awkward and fearful around girls. The vicious verbal onslaught from my internal bully beat down my thoughts. They would blurt out, *You're going to mess up, and she's going to laugh at you. You're such a dork. Besides, she's too good for you.* The constant negative thinking began to build day by day, layer by layer, beating me down. These strong emotions flooded my brain, flooded my body. I didn't know how to act or feel. I was constantly doubting myself around my friends and peers. What I didn't realize was the anxiety was morphing into something darker, and it eventually morphed into depression. The doubt turned to pain, followed by the need to run from my fears, becoming numb. Self-loathing quickly followed, and my negativity was reinforced by my internal bully. It became difficult to manage being around anyone.

HINDSIGHT—LOOKING BACK

Anxiety sucks. Depression sucks. Being in public and being surrounded by people sucks. It feels like the walls are closing in on me. My hands sweat profusely, my ligaments and muscles tense up, the fight or flight syndrome kicks in, and my brain goes into full panic mode as it wants to force my body to run as fast as I can from the situation like The Roadrunner. These nasty, mini anxiety attacks happen a good portion of the time I go out in public. I continue to force myself to go out to break the anxiety, with little positive results. One comfort I've learned over the years is that I'm not the only one struggling with these anxious moments. Nearly twenty million Americans suffer anxiety issues. It helps me not feel alone because when I was younger that was all I felt. I felt alone, scared, and terrified.

Stories of these anxious moments are often included in my speeches when I'm describing how I intentionally failed college courses so I wouldn't have to speak in front of my classmates. Another story that I occasionally talk about in my speech was the semester I took an interpersonal communications class. I took it online so I wouldn't have to talk to people. Yet, for some strange reason, here I am standing in front of hundreds of thousands of people, telling my darkest moments, pouring my heart out to complete strangers. Most of the time, I get a subtle laugh from the crowd when I tell these stories. I've overcome my anxiety and fear of public speaking for my career. I'm proud I've done that, but it doesn't end there. The elation of being on stage quickly disappears when I go out in public. My reality hits me when I try to finish workouts, go to the grocery store, or worse, when I avoid net-working events. I often close my eyes, visualizing the numerous missed opportunities lost from anxiety, being fearful, too shy, too scared about integrating with others, preventing me from taking full advantage of certain opportunities, all because I haven't been able to conquer my social anxiety and fear of being in public.

We can develop tools and methods to help control and shift our anxious thoughts. You will have to conquer other anxieties and con-quer other fears. Once you beat one battle, another battle waits in the wake, waiting to be hit head-on and conquered. It's an ongoing challenge of growth as a person. Being uncomfortable until you are comfortable is all about facing your fears. I've tried, I've overcome, I've tried again and failed, often failing miserably. But I will lick my wounds, isolate from others, regroup, still be fearful for a while, but will try again, then again, and again until I can overcome my anxiety at some point.

Anxiety, negative self-talk, the wrong or misplaced priorities, and living in this disastrous world of comparisons, mainly due to social media platforms, are large bricks in your foundation. If you struggle like I do with any of the anxiety, negative self-talk, depression, or other mental health issues and don't address them when you are young, they will only lead to eventual cracks in your foundation in the years to come. If your fears and isolations are not counseled and maintained, these cracks will grow into much bigger problems. By addressing anx-iety and that inner voice, we can alter the future of how each individ-ual faces fear later in life. It takes hard work, consistency, dedication.

But just like most things, your fears can be limited and curtailed by addressing the foundational bricks of anxiety, negative self-talk, and social media comparison.

CHALLENGE YOURSELF

I recently moved to Houston, Texas, after my divorce. I needed to get out of Colorado. Every car at a stoplight that looked like my ex-wife's was sending me into a crying tailspin. So, I moved. Packing up everything I owned, I took off on a new journey with my dogs—my best friends. Not knowing a soul in Houston has been isolating and a lonely process trying to rebuild my life over again.

To challenge my anxiety, I forced myself to attend a networking event in order to meet new people, and it nearly caused me to have a full-on panic attack. I almost left the moment I entered the parking lot. Sitting in my car, I took a few deep breaths and told myself I needed to do this and face my anxiety and fear of groups of people. The walk to the doors of the building from my parked car was nerve-wracking, my heart was racing, and I had thousands of thoughts about turning around and heading back to the car—it continued through check-in. Once I checked in, I didn't go meet people. In a panic, I headed straight to the bathroom, trying to regroup, nearly leaving the building when I came back out. I was fighting my negative thoughts and internal conflict of panic. I breathed deeply, calming myself down enough to find a seat quickly and quietly in the back of the room. It was an uncomfortable situation, but just like facing most fears, the fear receded and slowly dissipated, and I eventually made it through the event unscathed. I ended up making a few good connections and heard about a great organization that I would eventually volunteer for.

Challenge yourself to step out of your comfort zone and make a new friend. When I say a friend, I mean somebody in person, not on social media or over the phone. Build a new relationship with somebody at school or the gym, go to a networking event and meet people who are of like minds. Slowly break the fear, one conversation and situation at a time.

Journal your anxieties and fears. Write down your fears on a piece of paper and get them in front of you. Read them slowly and out loud. In doing so, ask yourself, "Am I really afraid of this? What will happen if all things fall apart?" or "What will happen if I actually face this anxious moment?"

Write down a list of ten moments in your life where fear was present. Out of the ten anxieties you wrote down, which ones did you overcome? Spend a moment and reflect. Was the anxiousness internally created by how you were raised and programmed?

CHAPTER 9

THE BATTLE OF VOICES (SELF-TALK) AND THE ORIGIN OF DOUBT

Should I be embarrassed to admit that I have constant battles with my internal voices? Yes, I have voices that whisper to me in my 7-1/8 hat-sized head. I'm not embarrassed to admit I hear a voice or two in my head. Do you have similar voices inside yourself, guiding and influencing your thoughts? Let's address the elephant in the room before we go any further. Guess what? You are not crazy! I know I'm not crazy for hearing a voice either. This is something I lacked as a youth, which, in turn, made me feel crazy. I wish I would have known that it was completely normal to have an inner dialogue and not be crazy. Today, I'm fully aware and cognizant of my inner monologue and my inner voice. Over the years, I've learned to decipher which voice to listen to. My inner voice is obviously silent to others but can be very loud to me, telling me how I should respond to any given situation. Disclaimer: I'm not schizophrenic, and these are not schizophrenic voices either; there is a big difference between internal dialogue voices and actual voices.

Growing up watching cartoons in the early 1980s, my TV was inside of a wood chest-like box. To get any TV stations, we would need to adjust the rabbit ears or antennas that were made with tin foil or old wire coat hangers. The rabbit ears were pointed high into the sky, attached by some faulty wiring attached to a large metal antenna on top of the roof. Many of my memories growing up were of my dad cussing and slamming doors every time he wanted to watch something on TV. It was something of a spectacle hearing his cussing outside as he climbed the ladder to get on top of the roof. His teeth would make this gritting sound, kind of like fingernails scraping a chalkboard, when trying to watch something. It didn't matter if there was a windstorm or snowstorm, angrily my dad would get on top of the roof and adjust the antenna. Looking back at those times, my father was risking his body for four measly TV stations (2, 4, 7, 9). No matter how perfectly he thought he aimed the giant antenna into the Colorado sky, black and white ants of static would still run across the screen. Today's kids always have 4K videos at hand with access to nearly anywhere they desire to watch something. Times and technology have changed incalculably since I was a kid.

Back to the cartoons I watched as a kid. These cartoons would show a power struggle in nearly every episode. The main character was stuck in a predicament, facing a crossroads with some monumental, pivotal decision, most often at a critical point in the episode. Then, abruptly, in a puff of smoke, two new characters appeared on opposing shoulders. On one shoulder, an angel-like figure appeared, dressed in a white robe and halo around its head, sometimes wearing angel wings. The halo figure in white confidently preached, "You know what you should do. Make the right decision. It's the right thing to do." Seconds later, the shady red robe-wearing character on the other shoulder voiced the opposite sentiments. The shady character whispered to choose the dangerous, exciting path, almost always the opposite of what was right, even if it meant it was the wrong choice. Both voices were on full display, showing the truth about our inner voices that we have.

This type of scene is prevalent in most of our lives. We are all faced with countless choices to make—often hearing multiple inner voices and inner directions on what impending choice we should make. In my case, the white-robed positive inner monologue tells me to follow the game plan, to follow the script that is laid out, do what is right, and continue to be a good human being. Faith in the positive choices through difficult times is what I've wanted to embrace since 2004. All I have is faith. What I do understand is that the more I listen to the white-robed voice, the more positive choices I make day in and day out. The more positive aspects in life begin showing up. It's downright difficult to always choose that positive inner monologue and have no idea where my future is taking me because that second, negative voice seems to ooze out confidence with exciting, thrilling, and often easier choices at that moment. The second voice on my shoulder often feeds and influences my impulsivity. Acting and reacting to my wildly up-and-down roller coaster of emotions as a manic-depressive. This voice takes me away from the game plan. It's my alter ego. This second voice tends to put me in troubling times, loudly persuading me and reiterating over and over, *You are E-FISH. E-mutherfucking-Fish. You can be a bad man*—a Muhammad Ali-type voice plays out in my head—*when you let go of your restraints and let loose. Screw the game plan. Let's go out and party, enjoy life. You are going to die anyway, might as well go out with a bang,* as if feeding off the impulsive energy monster residing inside my body. The old me loved that voice. *Drink this, pop this, smoke this, be free, screw all these lame-ass people who never experience anything. It's time to enjoy life.* I'm no longer that person, but that voice still shows up, attempting to persuade me to be the old me. It's been difficult fighting that negative voice over and over for years—and the fight still rages on. This is a lifetime battle I have yet to conquer.

NEGATIVE VOICE WINS

My time in elementary school was easy. Only a handful of times did I ever worry about what people cared, thought, or said about me. Most of the time, I was completely oblivious to others' concerns or judgments. My childhood brain was evolved just enough to pass through school, even though I was socially awkward, shy, quiet, and timid. I still enjoyed my life and who I was. My frontal lobe would develop later—much later—than most of those I grew up around. It didn't take long before I realized that my natural ability in sports was my social platform. Sports was my equalizer. My ability to play nearly every sport, from soccer, baseball, football, basketball, swimming, wrestling, track, golf, and other small games, helped me breeze through elementary school. Something changed on the first day of seventh grade. My life began to turn for the worse when I hit middle school. A cataclysmic, defining moment in my life took place. It was the moment where my confidence as a kid was first torn into pieces, then shattered like a piece of glass dropped from the roof of a skyscraper, and finally stepped on for pleasure. Mind you, I was already a shy and emotionally stunted kid, behind nearly everyone in my grade. The little confidence and ego I had was earned from sports. That social readiness and confidence vaporized into thin air. The origin of my negative self-image and low confidence was created and ignited at this very moment, eventually leading to much more devastation and destruction in my life.

The day of seventh-grade orientation, kids from all over the district would meet each other for the first time. The anticipation was scary going from elementary school into the big, bad junior high. At some point during the orientation day, students were in groups and told to use icebreakers to meet the kids from other schools. This already had me on edge. The group of girls next to my group consisted of girls who went to my elementary school and a couple of new ones from the other district elementary schools. The icebreaker was over, and they were talking about other things when suddenly I heard the new, pretty, and very popular girl say out loud, "You dated him? Gross." It didn't take long to realize that comment was in response to the only girl I "dated" in sixth grade, as she seemingly shook her own head in disgust. An instant switch went off inside my mind, turning my head into a thought loop of negative self-talk and chatter for the entirety of my life. "You dated him? Gross."

From that moment, the voice of doubt, fear, and lack of social confidence was deeply planted and rooted into the recesses of my brain.

My conscience ignited from an innocent child to a universal explosion into adolescence. It was my "big bang" of the real world and real life; the concept of popularity matriculated in an instant. A whispering voice of doubt instantly took residence in my adolescent mind. An enemy existing inside my own mind, ready to fight me every day of my life, began taking ownership of the decisions I made. My bully was not some older kid in school dunking my head in a toilet. My bully was my own internal voice. Fear and doubt came from my own negative thoughts. My inner voice became the biggest, meanest, tormenting bully on the planet, constantly belittling and whispering, *You're ugly, not good enough. They are making fun of your looks. You're ugly.* The negative self-talk became uncontrollable.

This defining moment in the middle school gym should have been so insignificant in the grand scheme of life, but that's not how it works for an impressionable pre-pubescent teen. It ultimately became a large piece of my foundation. My negative self-talk and destructive internal dialogue were created. The small cracks in my mental foundation were just hit by an earthquake, causing those small cracks to become gigantic ravines in my life's self-confidence with regard to girls, dating, and the need to be cool.

HINDSIGHT IS ALWAYS 20/20

Constant failure seems to follow me no matter how many good choices I make, but I've learned how to do a decent job managing my negative thinking. By no means have I conquered it. This battle with my negative thoughts will be ongoing until the day I die. I wish I would have addressed these issues in middle school, but I didn't, and now I'm faced with the unintended consequences of my lack of mental health counseling as a teen for the rest of my days. Negative self-talk can alter and destroy your entire life if not managed appropriately. It doesn't matter if you are a middle/high school kid struggling through life or in college with the world as your oyster. You can be an adult with a great job, happy family, and normal 9–5 life but still be meandering through the normalcy of life, dreading the day with negative thinking that will eventually lead to negative actions. The smallest seed of doubt and negative self-talk can destroy your confidence, preventing you from obtaining your goals and your purpose in life.

Positive thinking and positive self-imaging create a new positive energy. The great thing about creating a positive self-image is you need nobody. This is a mental exercise, a practice, a game that you can do alone. When you are alone and dealing with negative thoughts is when this is the most important.

Over the years, I've developed a habit of not allowing my negative thoughts to control my life. I have bad days where the negative self-talk attempts to beat down my inner confidence. I've developed habits centered on managing my mental health, learning to force most of the negativity and doubt out of my thought process. I did a fantastic job at fighting the negative thoughts away until March/April-ish of 2021. Something broke inside. I began allowing negative thoughts to infect my life, leading to doubt, isolation, and loss of faith in my marriage. This seepage of negativity led to the worst moment in my life when my wife asked for a divorce months later. It was as if my brain shut off and I could no longer produce any positive thoughts. I felt possessed by the negative black cloud of despair and unwavering pit of depression. The darkness of my thoughts and the resulting energy-sapping destroyed my life. Now, I'm suffering the consequence of listening to that negative voice on my shoulder.

CALL TO ACTION

A few basic steps to improve your own self-talk.

The simplest yet most difficult step is to stop saying negative things to yourself over and over. If you can catch yourself thinking, *I'm not good enough* or *I can't do that,* stop yourself right away, count down from five, and refocus on something you are good at. Counting down from five will stop your negative thought loop from happening.

If I can consistently catch myself from becoming trapped in a negative thought loop, I remind myself that I truly believe I can do nearly anything I put my mind to. The key is to catch myself before it's too late.

Here is a brief example of my positive self-talk when things are not going as planned.

I'm changing lives. I'm inspiring the youth, helping corporations build better futures. I literally save lives from alcohol use, drug use, and completing suicide. How fucking cool is that? I tell myself these sayings when I'm struggling with that seed of doubt. When these positive things I do come back into my thought process, I begin to smile. The resounding strength of negative thinking dissipates, and I feel much better.

On days when that negative mindset is persistent, go somewhere quiet and write down a list of five to ten positive thoughts, goals, and things you are grateful for. Don't type or text them on your phone, iPad, or laptop. Handwrite them down in a little notebook. There is scientific evidence that shows handwriting creates a certain boost in focus and an ability to remember what you physically wrote down. You can even use a dry-erase board, but manually write the statements out. These are your positive self-talk mantras.

Here are a couple of mine that I've been using since I became a keynote speaker. *I will be the best speaker I can be. I will change millions of lives!* It's graduated to, *I will be the most booked speaker on the planet. I will be the most booked speaker on the planet.*

When I write these down, I believe they will come true. Even seeing these statements right now as I edit this section of the book has provided a sense of well-being as a large smile shows on my face, and I realize the importance of my life. I'm alive to help and serve others. I'm alive for a reason. I'm not here just to survive; I'm alive to thrive by changing the lives of others. (*Psst...*I feel better already.)

When I write my lists of the positive things in my life, it forces me to smile. After I speak and do events, a rush of joy comes over me when

I get back to the hotel. Helping others brings me joy. The ability to see others change their lives from my story or one of my workshops somehow helps alleviate the weight those individuals have been carrying. Once they voice their struggles, you can see the weight of the world vaporize off their shoulders. It's amazing to see. I use these moments of pure joy as "tools in my toolbox." On my bad days, I think of the moments I help others, and it turns my negative self-talk into positive affirmations of redemption, to me—success.

CHAPTER 10

INFLUENCERS AND TOMFOOLERY

"Comparison is the thief of joy."
- UNKNOWN

Let's face it: the world is influenced 24/7/365 by an endless barrage of media that tends to dominate our world. These platforms like Instagram and TikTok have billions of active users/viewers. We live in a world where users voice their opinions with little to no credibility, while others are re-posting stories, articles, and news that might include disinformation or "fake news." Sifting through the information and determining the credibility is left to the viewer's own devices. It's up to the user's ability to sift out what is real and what is phony. The problem is, many users have no idea what is real and what is fake anymore, believing everything they see and read, creating this large population who is misinformed about the reality of the world. I'm not bashing or standing on either side of the political fence—heck, I've been caught up in news that I thought was real and it ended up being a bunch of tomfoolery.

We have all been influenced by some type of outlet, platform, medium, or by our friends and family. Every TV show, NBA playoff, or Super Bowl is inundated with commercials. The world is one big platform, everyone vying for opportunities to influence others. Advertising, influencing, and marketing is how the Western world's economy operates. It's now rooted in to our population's societal norms. The type of clothes you wear, shoes you buy, and social status are influenced by the type and cost of the cell phone in your pocket. Keeping up with the Joneses seems to be an even bigger issue now from social media, and the negative effects are becoming more and more apparent.

It's hard to fathom the pressure on the youth and this generation with social media. Our world is consumed with images, videos, likes, hearts, and emojis on Facebook, Twitter, Instagram, Snapchat, YouTube, and any other social media platforms, websites, or apps that are methodically maneuvering the tech waves, invading all our lives like a virus. Our path to image and video consumption is projected to increase year-over-year. According to Phututorial, there have been 12.4 trillion photos taken throughout human history. By 2030, this number will increase to 28.6 trillion, more than doubling within the next seven-plus years. Over 1.72 trillion photos are taken worldwide every year, and it will continue to increase into the near future.[2] Our society is a glutton for visual stimulation, all of which are on the platforms we follow. Images and video have quickly become the lifeblood in this world of comparison we live in, and it's not going anywhere. It's only going to get worse, according to the numbers above.

Billions of dollars are spent by businesses and corporations on advertising and marketing to influence the buying decisions of end-users. It's not just the businesses and corporations shelling out dollars, it's even individuals, solopreneurs, bloggers, and vloggers living out of a van. They will spend thousands of dollars to market themselves as social media influencers, content creators, and life coaches. So-called "influencers" will empty their diminishing bank accounts with the hopes of making it big with their cheesy-ass videos, or marketing products, services, "how-to" videos, and courses offered on their social media platforms for audiences. I loathe this "gold rush" and despise it. You can say I'm a hater because others are successful at it and I'm not, but I don't even try to be.

Parents need to know the impact social media has on their kids and what type of negative correlations follow. Teens emulate what they see. "Students who saw images of partying with comments posted by friends were about twenty percent more likely to become drinkers or smokers themselves over the next few months," according to the Journal of Adolescent Health.[3] Youth are already easily influenced and impressionable to begin with. Adding the negative energy vibrating through the social atmosphere is lightly dripping kerosene on a small fire. Just like any fire, it typically starts small and is controllable, but when excess fuel is added to the flames, or the faster the drip flows, the faster the fire grows. The same goes for the use of social media. It starts slowly for many and ends up consuming their lives.

Social media has increased mental health issues in teens and even adults. It's caused increases in suicide and bullying. There is a direct correlation between social media and an increase in suicide, depression, anxiety, and other various mental health issues. In the U.S. alone there was a twenty-five percent increase in suicide attempts among teenagers between 2009 and 2017—the years when social media began to take shape and root its addictive tentacles into our society. Furthermore, findings from a population-based study show a decline in mental health in the U.S., with a thirty-seven percent increase in the likelihood of major depressive episodes among adolescents.[4] Social media contributes heavily to the issues behind the world of comparison in which we live today. People tend to want what others have, and it doesn't help that technology has given users twenty-four-hour access to those who display that they are living fabulous lives. We compare, wishing we had the same, ultimately causing depression and anxiety after feeling inadequate for what we lack.

Full disclosure: I loathe social media. Yet I'm addicted just like the millions of others. I'm addicted far more than I'd like to admit. I'm an addict to picking up the phone, glancing at the screen as if I'm missing out on an important email or some irrelevant post from a speaker I follow, or maybe a direct message from a student. My biggest vice is basketball videos. I can watch highlights, moves, training videos, podcast interviews, and clips from *Inside the NBA* on TNT and not even realize I've just wasted hours of my day. It's addictive, especially when you rationalize in your head that it's okay because you are "learning" something while you drool on yourself and your thumbs are hurting from scrolling over and over all while looking at that stupid screen in the palm of your hands. I also rationalize that it's important to me as a keynote speaker to understand the latest trends, articles, blogs, and videos of the demographics and audiences I'm trying to help. I rarely post videos or have much of a presence online, again rationalizing that it's okay to pick my phone up to see what's going on in the world since I'm not posting over and over, so it's not consuming me like everyone else. That's a bold-faced lie. It's consuming me. I want to stop picking up my phone (upwards of one hundred times per day). I need to stop, but I can't. It's an addiction just like caffeine, smoking, drinking, or drugs. It alters the mind, changing how the chemistry in my brain works. For all the blatant disgust I talk about social media influence, I'm a walking contradiction.

Let's face it: this book is just another way to promote my business, another way of creating my influence, allowing me another platform to later be used on social media and marketing for speaking gigs. It's another way I can provide value to people through my story to help others. But don't get me wrong, I don't really want to write a book or be more involved with marketing and promotion—I'm sick of it all, but it's a necessary evil for me to speak. If I could do two hundred speeches at schools a year and never post a picture or video again and still have the same impact I do now, I would never post again. I know I'm going to have to promote this book, do social media posts about how great I think it is, or how great I think I am, which I think I am. Yes, I have an ego; anyone on stage has one, and any speaker that tells you they don't are lying! But I don't want to promote or feel that I need to tell or show everyone. KISS—keep it simple, stupid. I just want to travel from school to school, event to event, and avoid having to sell anything. That's not why I began speaking.

HIERARCHY INFLUENCE

Over the years, I've had hundreds of conversations with parents about how to talk to their children about mental health. Why? Parents are often misinformed themselves about mental health and the risk factors associated with a mental health issue. Parents often think they did something wrong, placing all the blame on themselves for the issues their child might have. Parents carry the guilt, believing they raised their child wrong, hurting their ego in the process, potentially causing their own depression and anxiety issues. Mental health has been taboo for so long, parents don't want other parents to know their child is suffering from a mental health issue.

A few years back, I had a friend whose daughter attempted to take her own life in high school. The mother's circle of friends found out that her daughter was suicidal, and they all stopped talking to her. They ousted her and her daughter from the school social hierarchy. In a time of need, the circle of friends ran. It's disappointing and disgusting how those friends treated my friend's family—they should be ashamed. But again, that is the negative stigma around mental health. It's such a hard topic that friends are willing to lose friends if a child is struggling with depression or suicidal ideation.

Broaching the subject of alcohol, bullying, drugs, peer pressure, and sex with their children is difficult for parents. Parents, whether they realize it or not, influence their kids' morals, values, and habits. Kids will emulate their parents' influences and carry them into their own adult lives. Children follow what their parents do. A poor choice by the parent will influence their children to likely make many of the same mistakes. First-time parents are flying by the seat of their pants—trial-and-error—in how they raise their offspring. Depending on how they were raised, that is likely how they will raise their kids. If the parent was raised to not believe in the importance of mental health, they will teach their kids not to believe in the importance of mental health.

It's not just teens, parents, and family settings that are influenced. It starts at the top. For generations, the bottom line has been all that matters in the corporate world. High-level executives have been trained to work their employees as hard as they can to drive up the profit, and in return, take a nice fat performance bonus check along the way. We reward people for pushing their company to new levels each year, pleasing the stakeholder's confidence in the direction the leadership is taking them. Ruling by the iron fist has worked in the past, but it is slowly moving away from the go-to philosophy. Caring for your employees and treating them as assets has begun planting its roots into the corporate norm. The next step is to add alcohol, substance abuse, and mental health training into organizations and watch the bottom lines flourish even more.

The amount of pressure to outperform one another, to get that new corner office, new job title, or chasing a new paycheck is negatively impacting one's own health and family dynamics. Pressure often leads to alcohol and substance use in employees in a cover-up of their untreated mental health issues. Leadership needs to address these issues and influence and encourage their employees to take care of themselves. Employees are the most important asset a company can have outside of its intellectual property (IP). Without healthy employees who believe in the mission, the IP can only get a company so far. Suicide costs the business economy upwards of $490 billion per year due to lost work production and healthcare costs.[5] As I say in my workshops, "If I haven't touched you in your head or your heart by now, then let me hit you in the pocketbook." Suicide, alcohol, and drugs not only destroy lives but also greatly decrease the bottom line for millions of businesses and companies. Suicide has skyrocketed in the work demographic job force. Data shows that roughly seventy percent of all suicides are by twenty-five to sixty-four-year-olds, which are the working laborer force. Diving deeper, males make up fifty percent of the population but account for nearly eighty percent of all suicides, four times the rate of females.[6] Three-quarters of all suicides in the United States are grown adults who are pressured to succeed at any cost, even if those costs are their very lives. To the middle-aged adults who picked up this book: you are the vast majority of where the problems exist versus the kids my keynote presentations currently focus on. This is the reason why I pursued writing this book. The last decade has been spent speaking to and inspiring the youth, saving and changing their lives. This is my favorite thing in this world—there is nothing greater for me to do at this point in my life—but as I grow and expand my career, I will be branching out into the corporate world because of the sheer numbers of those struggling who I can help. It's you the reader, it's you the parent, the worker, the business owner, the adult who has been misled by the myth that they are supposed to have this life figured out. You don't have to have life figured out. Life is difficult at any age. My challenge to you is to make a single choice each day to improve on the day before. Your life will improve in a short time, better than yesterday, and much better than a year ago. All you need to do is strive to improve one percent each day by making one single choice to better yourself. That's it—one choice every day!

PEOPLE COME AND GO

During the question-and-answer sessions after my keynotes, I'm often asked about my friends from middle school and high school. In my profession, I try to be as honest as possible. I believe it's one of my jobs to convey the truth about specific situations like my anxiety in school. I tell students just how little importance middle school and high school friendships truly mean in most cases. I try to describe how all the anxiety, depression, and stress I had socially and in making friends in school means nothing in the big scheme of life. During my time as a student, I constantly worried about what people thought of me or what they said. I was driving myself crazy with thousands of thoughts about seeking acceptance, when it doesn't matter in the long-term. But as a student, you don't think about the future, only the now. I tell audiences all the time that nobody I worried about impressing in middle school is even on my radar today. They are Facebook acquaintances. If it wasn't for social media, I wouldn't even think about them or care what in the world they are doing. I'm not trying to be mean, as those friends on my Facebook reading this book are now thinking, "Damn, Fish is a dick. Who does he think he is?" If that is you, ask yourself, "If it wasn't for Facebook, would I have even thought about Fish?" If it wasn't for my career of being a speaker, would you even care what I am doing? Would you want to reach out and grab lunch with me? Here's a question to help determine how close we are. How many of you knew about my accident and how many reached out? Trust me—I know how many. How many of you wrote letters while I was incarcerated? That's easy for me. I charted every single letter I received and every single letter I wrote, plus the dates received and sent out. How many of you knew of my marriage? A handful of people. How many of you knew about my divorce? Just a handful. If you didn't know about either of those, we are not friends. We are social media acquaintances. I've seen ten or so people from middle school and high school not by accident or dumb luck. If I haven't reached out to you, that means we didn't have a real friendship. So why would I lie to the students I try to help?

The reality is friends come and go. Consider yourself lucky if you had a constant friend through school. Very few are lucky enough to have that in their lives and they are blessed if they did. I wish I had a true group of friends that I could have grown up with, but I'm kind of an outcast and not good at friendships. Life happens, people move on, families move on, friends move on—it's the reality that young people fail to realize. I wish I would have realized in middle school that none of the anxiety and self-shame of peer pressure would actually matter, even though every second of every day I was self-conscious of what people thought of me walking those halls at my middle and high schools. Those anxious times in my life still impact me today. I should have influenced myself toward chasing my dreams versus worrying about what others thought of me.

CALL TO ACTION

You are the sum total of the five closest people in your life. Meaning the five people you associate with most have the biggest influence on who you are and how you act. Who do you allow to influence you? Are your influences on social media? Is it your family or friends? Choose wisely.

Take an honest inventory of the five people you spend the most time with.

Ask yourself these questions:

- Are they positively impacting me?
- Do they want the best for me?
- Are they genuinely helpful or hurtful in my quest to be a better person?
- Do they push me in a positive direction or are they always negative?
- Am I a better person when I'm around them or do I act out in ways I regret later?

If you can answer these honestly and without bias, you should be able to determine if these five people are beneficial for you or not. If they are not, you need to restructure your friend groups and those you spend the most time with. I've pushed many friends away for this very reason. Since the accident, I don't hang out or spend time with anyone I grew up with. I choose very carefully who I allow into my life—and in all honestly, I've made my circle too small. And that is something I need to work on.

CHAPTER 11
IT WON'T HAPPEN TO ME

"Optimism is good. Too much of it can be damaging."
– KAVI ARASU

Your social status, job status, or number of zeros in your bank account doesn't exclude you from the likelihood of struggle or a traumatic event. Everyone in the world will experience some type of traumatic event. Right now, you are thinking, "You're telling me everyone on the planet faces a traumatic event?" Yes. Think about all the car accidents you've seen, divorces you've heard about or maybe even been through yourself, considering over fifty percent of marriages end in divorce. Did you grow up in a single-parent household? What about your family and friends losing their jobs during the pandemic? All the alcohol and drug-related physical and sexual assaults that occur every hour of the day? What about the countless other crimes against humanity that affect us? These are all events that can greatly impact a person and alter their current path and/or future self.

The most common traumatic event that will take place for everyone is death—everybody dies at some point. Your entire family will be wiped off this earth, all the sons and daughters will die, all the parents will die, and for some, they already have. I hate to sound so morose, but this is life, and every living, breathing being on this planet will die. Death is a traumatic event for anyone. All these situations can shake even the strongest person's foundation.

We live in a world of trauma. Going back to your foundation and state of mental health is critical to your growth and learning how to persevere and be resilient in a season of struggle. We will all struggle at some point. Our foundation must be solid, prepared through awareness, and educated with numerous resources or tools to be prepared for life's battles. Often, struggles come because we believe nothing bad can or will happen to us, especially if we are confident in the choices we make every day.

Nobody grows up wanting to be an alcoholic or addict. Addictions and poor behaviors/habits start out small, snowballing out of control if not paid attention to. Alcoholics and addicts don't take a sip of alcohol or use a prescribed Percocet saying to themselves, "I can't wait to be addicted." They are under the impression they can have a drink, take a prescribed pill, and stop when they need to. The scary thing is millions of alcoholics and addicts are led down the wrong side of addiction due to this unintended path of destruction.

Never in my life did I think I'd be an alcoholic or addict, yet I am, even though I haven't touched alcohol since 2004. I know beyond a shadow of a doubt I cannot take a sip or my life will be over as I know it today. I'll ruin my speaking career. Eventually, I'll walk down a very dark path into blackout drinking, loss of career, and countless other things. Drinking would literally be the worst decision I could make. I'm proud I recognize that, and I have drawn the line in the sand. I've lost loved ones over this hard line. I've made a conscious choice to avoid as many situations and people that regularly consume alcohol as possible, taking out any possible situation where alcohol can impact my life, even if I don't drink a sip. Avoiding people who are drunk is a huge foundational piece to keeping my sobriety for nearly twenty years. It's what I need to do to protect my own mental health. I'm content with my decisions.

THE LIQUOR COMES A-KNOCKING

Alcohol didn't knock on the front door of my life and politely say, "Hello. Let me introduce myself. I'm alcohol. Can we hang out for just the day?" as is the case for many capable social drinkers who are not alcoholics. In my case, the chemical composition of alcohol kicked down my door violently, spewing obscenities, ready for a battle, demanding and screaming at the top of its lungs, "DRINK ME! We will be best friends forever. I love you and you'll love me!!!" Alcohol quickly became my suitor and companion, a guest that wouldn't leave my system until I hit rock bottom. Alcohol and I spiraled out of control (next chapter) into a life-changing moment of pain and regret. In any case, I never thought it would ever happen to me.

When I was in elementary school, I told all my friends that I would never drink or smoke cigarettes. I was adamant about not drinking alcohol or smoking cigarettes, saying no on plenty of occasions growing up. Was it because I wanted to play in the NBA and knew alcohol and drugs would ruin my chances? No, not at all. I witnessed one of my favorite people in the world die of alcoholism and cancer, my grandmother. When I saw her body in the casket, I remember telling myself—at the age of eleven or twelve—I would never do what she did and die of alcohol. My grandma's impact and passing were pivotal in my development—until I forgot what that moment felt like. At one point, I allowed my anger, frustration, and being surrounded by peers to alter my choices around alcohol. Unbeknownst to me, alcohol would become an addiction I couldn't shake off. It became especially difficult when I started using it as self-medication for my anxiety and depression. Eventually, drinking alone every night became my favorite thing to do. It got to the point that I needed to be drunk every night.

The origin of my first night of drinking should have been a sign that alcohol was going to be a problem for me. I should have listened to my internal dialogue: *Hold on; this is disgusting. Grandma passed away from this stuff. What are you doing?* The white robe voice was silenced by anger as the red robe voice on my shoulder was saying, *Dude, you just lost to the Lambkins* (crosstown rival in basketball—and I was pissed). *The girl you like is at the party. If you and her are both drunk, maybe you'll score.* I was a teenage boy with a high sex drive, yet I couldn't score with a chick to save my life. I began rationalizing that others were getting laid at parties so why couldn't I? For a skinny, shy, zitty, sixteen-year-old virgin, getting laid was on the agenda, and being drunk was the only way I believed I would "get lucky." The influencing voice of alcohol was playing on my male instinct to procreate, and the frustration and anger from losing to my cross-town rivals was the catalyst that influenced my decision to drink.

Listening to the wrong voice, things did not go as planned. At some point during the evening, you could find me passed out on a dirty bathroom floor, face, lips, nose, and every facial feature touching a piss-stained toilet bowl. Throwing up over and over with my friend on the left side of the toilet in the exact predicament I was in. It was as if we were playing tennis, volleying the tennis ball back and forth, but the ball was us puking our brains out. After each violent extraction and successful cleansing of our stomachs, a sound bite of "flush" was repeated over and over. I assume many of my adult readers have had similar nights like this if they've been drunk before—one of the negative consequences of alcohol that tends to get overlooked.

Little did I think that one night of drinking was going to lead me down a path of no return. Like I mentioned earlier, alcoholics and addicts don't drink or use the first night and think they have a problem. I should have known that damn near drinking an entire fifth of Jack Daniels by myself should have been a huge warning flag that I would have a problem. A hindsight of 20/20 would have been a great power back then, but I chose to drink and suffer the consequences from that one moment.

This story is not uncommon for millions of youths who drink for the first time and end up passed out, sometimes on toilets, in fields, strange rooms, or houses because they drank too much. If I were to ask you, the reader, to lay your head directly on the toilet, would you? Hell no. Just think about this: your skin touching the dirty toilet in some strange bar or apartment building. Lying on the floor with your head resting on the rim of the porcelain structure, with random people coming in and out, using the toilet before and after you flip the lid. Placing your head nearly inside the toilet bowl while you continue to vomit with your hands gripping the sides of the porcelain base. Then, upon completion of vomiting, you raise your hand toward the handle that has been touched by who knows how many dirty, unwashed drunkards' hands as you flush, wiping your mouth of the excess chunks of food from the day's earlier meal. Would you do that sober? Hell no. Yet millions of you have done exactly that. Alcohol tends to cause unintended moments like this in many amateur drinkers and continuously does it for the lifetime of a full-blown alcoholic. These types of situations tend to get overlooked for the thrill or desire to be drunk.

TRUTHS UNTOLD

Moments like my first night of drinking are never highlighted during the attractive and sexy TV advertisements for beer or alcohol. Airwaves promote only the fun side of drinking at a rate of $7.7 billion spent on alcohol advertising by the year 2023.[1] They never show commercials about the vomiting, addiction, or a once-innocent person losing everything they had in life for the liquid in a bottle. We don't see the endless number of fights and numerous relationships lost to drunkenness or domestic violence. We never see the marketing plan showing the vast number of people who cheat on their significant others while drinking and partying. Advertisements only show the fun side of drinking, never the destruction and sad outcomes. If liquor companies advertised and promoted the real-life alcohol-induced moments, a significant amount of youth might never start drinking in the first place. Heck, many adults would never drink. First-time drinkers and youth fail to realize the buzz only lasts for a limited time, then the horrible hangover happens, never thinking that it can become a problem in life. The lives of alcoholics often fall apart, leading to darkness and the abyss of depression, which is only one of the side-effects of drinking they never talk about.

There is a misconception where the media tends to portray those struggling and addicted to drugs, pills, or alcohol as losers, bums, scum, and the weak-minded. They are the underbelly of society. The media doesn't talk about the very successful people (who are not celebrities) who lose their lives or families every single day due to the impact of alcohol—many who were under the impression it would never happen to them. That is exactly what I told myself.

To put this in a much larger light, the World Health Organization reports that just under three million lives are lost each year to alcohol worldwide.[2] Let's repeat that again. Three million lives are lost each year by alcohol. The metro area of Denver has a population of about three million people. Imagine the entire population of Colorado's state capital being wiped out every year. Three million people is a larger population than the individual population of the USA's seventeen lowest populated states. We could combine the USA's four least-populated states, Wyoming, Vermont, Alaska, and North Dakota, and that would not even be the three million total lives lost.[3] I'll say it again: the population of those four states (and then some) dead annually. Alcohol destroys lives.

Happy hours, Christmas parties, NFL Sunday, and really any other day of the week are all opportune times for alcohol consumption. Business parties contribute heavily to the drinking issues in corporate America. According to the National Highway Traffic Safety Administration, about 1.5 million people are arrested each year for driving under the influence of alcohol or drugs. That means that one out of every 121 licensed drivers were arrested for driving under the influence.[4] Many of these impaired drivers are corporate Americans heading home after a business function that supplies alcohol. There are even numerous companies that have alcohol onsite and allow people to drink during working hours if it's not impacting the job or project.

According to the CDC, more than 140,000 people die from excessive alcohol use in the U.S. each year.[5] That is over three times, let me repeat that, three times more deaths than gun violence. More than 45,200 died in the U.S. from firearms in 2020.[6] Over 20,000 of those deaths are by the hands of the gun owner and are suicides, and many of those 20,000 are under the influence of alcohol at the time of taking their own lives. Does this change your thoughts about alcohol or maybe your stance on gun violence? It should.

If not, go sit in one of the thousands of AA rooms that are hosted in some free location at some dreary, cold, dark basement of a run-down building, church, or hospital. You will hear countless stories of people who had good-to-great lives, working a decent corporate gig, following the white picket fence life, climbing the corporate ladder, and moving upward to what a large portion of society dreams of as a perfect life from the outside looking in, only to lose it all after they became alcoholics and addicts.

Think about your current and past coworkers. Imagine roughly twenty percent of these individuals are silently dealing with some diagnosable mental health problem stemming from some difficult moment causing pain and trauma. Putting on a fake smile every day, nodding to you as they walk back into their cubicle, holding in the trauma of their divorce, holding in their pain of a legal issue, family problems, or health problems, and they tell nobody about it. Just imagine how many of these individuals are drinking or using drugs to forget about their trauma and move on in their life. They were casual users with no problems in the beginning. Then they begin to drink or use as self-medication, eventually developing a problem. It might seem like a scare tactic—well, it should—because this type of depressive addiction can eventually get to a point where they lose their job, lose everything. Excessive drinking causes companies major losses in productivity. The CDC reports that businesses lose around seventy-two percent of productivity from employees with alcohol issues from excessive drinking.

It also puts another eleven percent increase on the cost of healthcare, another ten percent on the cost of criminal justice cases, and another five percent of motor vehicle costs.[7] It costs insurance companies millions of dollars per year in drunk driving accidents. Specifically in my case, my parent's insurance company paid out close to $1.5 million for their umbrella policy, but a dollar amount does not make up for the loss of a life. I don't believe you can assign a financial figure on an individual's life, but insurance companies do just that. They have to, considering over 10,000 innocent lives are taken each year by drunk drivers.

Both men and women drink or use substances to hide their feelings; both men and women complete suicide. Alcoholism, drug addiction, and suicide are not sexist, and they don't discriminate by age or religion. As mentioned before, roughly seventy-five percent of the suicides in this country are by the workforce population, ages twenty-six to sixty-five. Out of those seventy-five percent, depending on the varying data and research out there, roughly sixty-nine to eighty percent of those suicides are by adult men. Research shows that men die by suicide at much higher rates than women.[8] Men are more likely to have access to handguns, pistols, or firearms, access to these instant killing weapons. It is the biggest reason why men have the highest rate of suicide. Women attempt to die by suicide at higher rates than men, but they choose to take pills to overdose or attempt to take their lives by cutting their wrists. These two common methods of attempted suicide are why more women survive. Why? Taking pills and cutting wrists are both methods of suicide that are not instantaneous like firearms. Yes, women can use handguns and take their lives, but the numbers and research show that this is mostly not the case. I'm so lucky I never owned a pistol or handgun. I know for a fact I wouldn't be here today. My attempts were always trying to overdose or drink myself to death, trying most nights to consume enough to pass into the afterworld. I'm grateful every day that I didn't die.

CALL TO ACTION

Take an honest inventory of your actions and ask yourself these questions.

- Do I have a drinking problem? Do I drink to hide my pain and sorrows? Or do I occasionally have a drink?

- Do I have a pill problem? Am I taking prescription pills that I don't need or shouldn't be taking from a friend or family member?

- Do I have an addiction to my phone? How many hours do I waste on my phone? Is it impacting my life?

If you can honestly answer these questions and recognize that you have a problem, there is help. Admitting and recognition is the first step to reaching a change. I know I had a drinking problem, and I know I cannot ever drink again. I recognize the problem and have worked hard to never go back.

CHAPTER 12

IT'S THE BOTTOM, AND YOU HAVE NOWHERE TO GO BUT UP

The force of rock bottom comes like a category 5 hurricane, slowly building up power and speed until the ensuing devastation follows. Weather channels broadcast information about the storm as it starts in the middle of the ocean, updating viewers that an impending swirl of destruction is heading toward the shore. Those watching the news or weather station can see the brightly colored Doppler radar highlighting the hurricane moving inland. Those living in the path of the hurricane board up their windows and brace for impact. Many hope and pray that ocean winds or undercurrents change the direction of the forthcoming destruction of the hurricane. Otherwise, they might have to evacuate. In some lucky moments, the hurricane does just that; it changes direction. Those who live on or near the coast avoid one-hundred-plus mile per hour winds, flooded streets, and power outages and can breathe easy another day.

Addiction and mental health rock bottoms are like the formations of hurricanes. A hurricane starts out as a small storm in the middle of the ocean and with the right conditions, grows bigger and stronger, moving closer and closer to the coast, much like a drinker or drug user when they first start to use and abuse. At first, the storm seems so far away and unlikely to account for much. Friends and family are the viewers of the media. From the outside perspective, those watching the news can see the crippling path of the hurricane coming, attempting to warn others in its projected path. They board up windows, fill the cabinets with non-perishable food, and buy gallons and gallons of water to survive days or weeks at a time. In the worst-case prediction, they prepare to evacuate. The addict is the powerful storm that is slowly forming, failing to realize the pending danger. They are unsuspecting of the dangerous power they are creating from their drinking and usage. Friends and family (TV viewers) can see the destructive path of the storm forming, often warning the addict that the winds are increasing, yet the user fails to recognize what's going on. They ignore any help offered. They are in denial that their rock bottom is gaining momentum toward the shore. They continue to use their alcohol or drug of choice, and suddenly—*wham*—they hit rock bottom with the force of a hurricane, destroying relationships and careers, along with many other unintended consequences of their choices around alcohol, drugs, and lack of mental health intervention.

OTHERS SPIRAL TOO

Rock bottom is a level nobody wants to reach, but many end up down there. Rock bottom claims the lives of 130 suicides per day in the USA, or roughly 47,000 suicides per year.[1] Then throw in another 107,622 lives lost from drug overdoses each year, and you have over 420 people per day dying at possibly the lowest moments of their lives. It's sad, and I believe many of those lives could be saved if society paid more attention and showed more care and love to those who are struggling.

Individuals are never taught how to survive or avoid hitting rock bottom. Society leads us to believe that only losers or scum will hit rock bottom. There is a misconception that normal people who live normal lives and follow all the societal norms will never hit rock bottom. There is a basic set of guidelines to avoid it: go to school, graduate high school; if you're lucky, go to college; if not, go to trade school;

or start working forty-plus hours a week; and as Eminem would say, "Don't do drugs." Seems simple. This appears to be the system our country is built on and trained for. Our workforce is created to have 9–5 jobs, emulating the same school system schedule. If you stray outside of these confines and rules, you are an outcast and susceptible to an unsuccessful life.

When people hit rock bottom, where do they go, who do they talk to, and how do they get out of it? I believe we need to educate more individuals on how to "embrace the suck," a common phrase used in the military. As a society, we can help individuals learn how to lessen the destruction their rock bottom causes and help them grow from it. Post-traumatic growth (PTG) is when an individual summons the strength to use a traumatic event as a launching pad for change and growth as a person. They use their rock bottom to catapult their lives into something powerful and successful. I look at it like this: when at the bottom, you have a clean slate to start over from scratch, creating a life that you want and desire.

I was completely unaware of the term or concept of PTG until a few years ago. I had lunch with somebody who explained what it was, and it made sense regarding who I'd become and where I was at my lowest. I believe this is where I learned to change and adapt to be the person I am today. I took my rock bottom and used it as a launching pad to a new life. I changed, growing from the worst moment in my life. If I can grow from such a horrible moment, why can't any other individual who hits rock bottom do the same?

As a society, we tend to shun those who struggle, rarely taking the time to dig deeper into why that individual hit rock bottom in the first place. We should be questioning why their respective rock bottom took place versus judging the individual for the result. In order to figure out how to prevent others from the same fate, we should ask some questions. Did this individual hit rock bottom because of a family incident where they were mistreated or sexually abused as a child? Did their parents go through a destructive, nasty divorce? Did the individual lose their job, lose their own business, or file for bankruptcy due to the global pandemic? These are all situations that are risk factors for mental health, which typically leads to self-medication of alcohol abuse and drug use. The 2020 National Survey on Drug Use and Health provides mental health and drug abuse statistics and reports that 52.9 million people in the USA age eighteen or older had a past-year mental illness, and seventeen million of these people had a coinciding substance use disorder[2], meaning they misused alcohol or drugs at the same time as their mental health struggles. Almost twenty million people are battling anxiety, depression, and other mental health issues at the same time they are battling an addiction. Mental health and addiction go hand-in-hand.

Being demoted or fired from a job—how does that make you feel? What about when a coworker you loathe lands the job you worked so hard for? Did they get the job over you because they have above-average ass-kissing skills? Does that cause you to feel more disdain for them? This is a pivotal moment to make a choice. Do you work harder to get the next opportunity or put your tail between your legs and quit? How long can you keep working harder? Days, weeks, months? What if it's years at the same job and still no promotion? Will you justify in your mind that it's okay to quit because you'll never get that promotion? The red robe voice in the mind says, *Screw this. I've been working my ass off and not getting seen. I'm done sacrificing and working this hard anymore.* Months go by as the quality of your work diminishes. Suddenly, management thinks you are hurting the bottom line. They realize you don't do anything to improve their company and fire you after never taking the time to figure out the underlying problem of why your work has declined. On top of that, your significant other wants a divorce and your kids hate you. The spiral is beginning and becomes out of control when you add alcohol and drugs to numb the pain, thinking this is the best way to cope. Months later, you're sleeping in a one-bedroom apartment, looking for jobs on Craigslist classifieds, and hate your life.

I've heard different versions of this story hundreds of times in AA rooms. It's more common than you think. A few of you are laughing at this situation, thinking it will never happen to you, and that might be true. You might have a loving family, a support system to help tread water and get back on your feet without missing a beat. You might have a level of resiliency that others don't have. Your mental fortitude kicks in and you never let yourself get that low because you have had rough experiences your entire life, so you deal with it. I applaud those who fit this grit and grind. Just imagine the larger percentage of people out there who lack any form of resiliency, those who have never had a bad thing happen to them. What do they do? They are lost, spiraling out of control because they've never been in this situation before. They hit rock bottom and find themselves in their small apartment with booze on their breath, questioning why or how they ended up there. It's not an uncommon story in AA rooms, rehabs, and prison facilities. All contain once-thriving lives lost by spiraling to rock bottom. This is far more common than you might imagine, and many in those dark, dingy rooms and jail cells had decent lives before the spiral began. People with families, and even great lives, who lost it all. Now they face the worst mindset they can imagine. What do they do, where do they go, and how do they handle their situations?

People tend to think post-traumatic stress disorder (PTSD) only impacts the military, and that's not the case. Millions of everyday people struggle with PTSD, ranging from individuals who experienced a car accident, divorce, domestic abuse; heck, I think countless people are dealing with PTSD from the pandemic. I know I am. Years later I'm still picking up shattered pieces of my life that blew up in my face when the world went into lockdown.

I'll use the military as an example because I want to use this book as my way of helping those who protect my freedoms and rights as an American. It's sad, the number of pressures the veterans experience and see, who often must relive their experiences in battle, losing platoon members and seeing bodies of innocent children, women, and men killed. Many of our vets come home with PTSD and turn to self-medication, ending in addictions and suicide.

PTSD also affects our firefighters, police personnel, and hospital workers. Imagine the scene of a police officer coming home after witnessing a drunk driving accident where an innocent man's life was lost and the driver was still alive and incoherent (in my case). These images are burnt on those police officers' brains for the rest of their days.

I've had an email conversation with one of the ex-cops from my accident who witnessed the pain I caused. I spoke to him over a decade after my accident, and that moment was imprinted on his brain, saying he couldn't forget that night and the scene of the crime. Just imagine how many other horrible scenarios he witnessed and is dealing with inside from his years of serving the community as a police officer. Do we ever take these moments into consideration and ask how that individual is doing? Maybe that is why he is no longer on the force and is a successful real estate agent (if you are looking for property in northern Colorado, I'll connect you). But seriously, tragic moments like these are never erased from the minds of the viewers, and they are traumatized for the rest of their lives.

HOW TO HELP THE YOUTH

The world is filled with chaos, destruction, accidents, and death. That is the reality of life. No matter the choices we make in life, accidents and death follow. My question is, how are schools preparing students to deal with these circumstances when they get older? Is it trial by fire? Or do we open the conversation and address these issues so they are better prepared and know what to do when this happens? We need to provide our young, and adults too, with the appropriate information and resources to seek help in a time of need. We need to help them realize trauma happens to millions every year, and they can get help.

We teach kids art, PE, math, and history, which are all needed for a child to find what they might like and be talented at. Yet, from what I have seen from the hundreds of schools that I have had the pleasure of speaking at, rarely do schools prepare their students for the social and emotional world in which we all live. I've never seen or heard of classes provided in K–12 or college about living through struggle. It's my belief that every person on this planet will face some type of struggle, and for some, that struggle will be the worst pain in their entire life. With the right awareness programs and education, we could potentially help prevent rock bottom before the downward trend or spiral even takes place. Awareness and preventive methods should be mandatory in schools. This would help students realize they are not alone, that everyone fails or struggles at some point in life. This would help the youth better understand so they don't feel worthless when they screw up. As adults, we know failure is a part of life. Kids don't. Second, it will help the youth realize their problems before they take place, helping them build tools of resilience to lessen the struggles and lessen the depths of a rock bottom, making it much easier to climb out when times get tough.

I think my speaking career is the greatest job on the planet; I love my career. I'm able to provide messaging and programming that will impact hundreds of thousands of lives. I'm humble enough to know my program is not a one-stop-shop and cure-all for prevention—I'm not that egotistical. What I do know is educational administrations need to provide stories or programs like Life CONsequences to their students multiple times per year. When I speak to administration officials, even if they don't book me to speak, I try to advise them to keep providing speakers and/or other programs in their schools on these types of life skill topics. They will save more lives than a geography test or history class—those are important topics to learn about, but not important enough to help in the survival of life.

This is one of my favorite statements by a principal. He told his entire middle school and high school at the assembly before I stepped on stage for the third time in six years, "You will learn more from Ethan's speech and his story than you will learn in any classroom this year."

One of the greatest testimonials you can receive from an educator in the system of over forty years.

A major takeaway from this book is to keep circling back to Part 1: The Foundation. Many of the individuals sitting in the basement rooms of AA, NA, or in those cold, constantly lighted prison cells lacked the appropriate awareness and education of what the consequences were and neglected their foundation and their mental health. Chances are highly likely that those struggling in those situations had no clue about mental health and the consequences they would face due to their unresolved issues and trauma.

How do we make a change? We start educating and promoting awareness at a young age so they are prepared for the problems and struggles in Part 2 that they are likely to face at some point in their lives, if they have not already experienced some type of family trauma already. Many of the struggles people will face (Part 2) typically take place when the person is unaware of how to prepare their minds to avoid or at least minimize and mitigate the risk of struggle. Awareness and education can prevent a massive spiral down.

During my divorce, it would have been very easy to spiral out of control. I had numerous opportunities to do so. The rock bottom spiral would have started with one choice in the wrong direction. It would have started with one drink, but I addressed my foundation, my mental health, and applied my own five keys for profound change. In doing so, I avoided unforeseen struggles and the potential for a significant spiral down toward a new rock bottom. I'm proud of how I managed my life, as I know with one sip of alcohol, my downward spiral will start all over again—I don't want that.

SUPPORT

One hundred percent, I would not be the person I am today if it were not for the support and love my family gave me growing up. They were a gigantic monolithic rock in my foundation. Their support was the reason I had the ability to handle the accident the way I did. The way they supported me from the moment they picked me up at the psych ward until coming out of the prison system three years later is a main reason for who I am today. Without their support, I would have chosen a different path during my incarceration and after my incarceration, ultimately changing who I am today. They were there in the worst of times and the best of times. No matter the distance I have from them right now, they will always be loved and appreciated.

PART 3
THE FIVE KEYS FOR PROFOUND CHANGE

This is *how* I changed.

Do you want a simple format to help change your life? These five basic concepts are what I've used to change from the drunk failure I was prior to 2004 to the speaker and author I am today. I use these five keys every day. When these five keys are applied correctly and timely, they help sustain a positive change in my life. Repeatedly, I will say I'm far from perfect, making countless mistakes along the way, just like everyone else. Yet when I use these five keys consistently, my life is significantly better. I'm in more control over the outcomes of my life. They are part of my daily routine, a path to success, and push me to constant forward progress. The global pandemic nearly ended my career and purpose. It ended my marriage because I didn't apply my five keys to it. I applied the five keys to my business life during the pandemic, but not my personal life. These five keys were the only reason I made it through the pandemic still intact as a speaker. Without them, I know I would have quit speaking, I would have quit writing this book, and I more than likely would have started drinking and quit my purposeful life. They saved my life, not just once, but on multiple occasions.

Applying these five keys to your daily routine will make your *foundation* stronger. Please understand, these are not some magic pill to take and all of a sudden the world becomes lollipops and gumdrops. That's not how life works. If utilized in the right manner, these keys will help you avoid significant struggles (Part 2). They will strengthen the most important aspects of your life. These keys will help you aim for and focus on success while boosting the resolve of your foundation. If you implement these simple keys into your days, you will see improvements in your life.

Whether it is my ongoing battle with mental health or past wars with alcohol, addiction, or living like a sardine trapped in the tight constraints of the Colorado prison system, being verbally screamed at during the Department of Corrections (DOC) boot camp or playing/coaching college basketball; starting my own businesses, failing financially, taking on loads of debt backing my various college degrees; enjoying accolades and receiving distinguished awards; experiencing the highs and lows of speaking, and now divorce—I will persevere through it all. My foundation relies on these five keys. They are instruments in my tool belt, and I'm ready for whatever this world throws my way. Through all the pain and struggle I've faced, I've learned how to remain resilient in difficult times—days of wanting to quit yet finding the faith to continue to push through obstacles for the greater purpose, chasing the vision that I see when nobody else does. These five simple keys are why I haven't given up in the darkest of times. All these experiences and moments are part of my journey. My mindset is to learn from each event and situation, no matter how hard they are at the time. All these significant chapters in my life provided moments to learn and grow from. Teaching is often the best way to learn, so here I am pouring out my life, my story, and the pains of my ever-evolving journey to you, the reader, at every stage I hit.

CHAPTER 13

KEY 1: CHANGE THROUGH ACCOUNTABILITY

There is no algorithm or formula for accountability to become a part of your life. I'm not promising you an instant change because there is no blue or red magic pill like in *The Matrix*. There is no magic saying that will instantly make this world easier. It takes dedicated discipline with exhausting amounts of focus to change, and not just a temporary change at that. We are talking about life-long, substantial change with levels of sustainability that many will not reach due to the amount of effort that change will take. If you, as a reader, can muster up and supply that type of energy day in and day out, you will unequivocally change. The reality is, *anyone* can change, and it starts with self-accountability.

Let's reiterate the secret sauce again from the beginning of this book. *Hard work* and the *desire* to change is the secret sauce. If you lack the ability to work hard, you will continue to struggle. If you lack the desire to change for yourselves and not others, you will struggle to make change. If you lack hard work and desire, then this book might not be suited for you. I'm not some guru promising instant change if you read my book. That would be a bold-faced lie. Please let me be as forthright and upfront as I possibly can with you—your situation and circumstance in life will not change until you can look at yourself in the mirror and honestly critique, reflect, and report back to yourself about who you are and what you represent. You and only you are accountable for the choices you make from this very moment moving forward. You can no longer blame your boss, your coworkers, your coaches, or your family for the life you have. You are who you are because of your choices! Until you can hold yourself accountable for the choices you have made or will make, things will unlikely change moving forward.

There are uncontrollable, Godly events that take place—storms, hurricanes, fires, accidents, a global pandemic. If you want the honest truth, there is always a choice that you made putting you into that situation. Example: I moved to Houston from Denver, Colorado, in June of 2022. I made a choice to move here. If a Godly act of a monsoon rainstorm takes place, flooding my home and leaving me homeless, it's my fault, not the weather's. I made the choice to move down here. I might complain about the heat, even get heat stroke, but I can't blame the weather. I chose to move to a city where triple digits are normal during the hot summer months. I am accountable for my decision to move here, no one else. There is no more time to put blame on others, as I can't blame others for my life. Take charge of your life, holding yourself accountable to it. Things will change when that happens.

WHEN IT ALL CHANGED

Accountability did not begin in the hospital after the accident when I realized the horrendous crime I committed. The responsibility for my actions did not take place while I was on a personal recognizance (PR) bond, awaiting sentencing for DUI vehicular homicide. My self-accountability didn't just appear every few weeks while nervously anticipating my attorney telling me what the judge was sentencing me to. My stomach dropped after the first call from my attorney saying, "Ethan, the judge is saying forty-eight years in prison, but I promise you that won't be your final sentence. We will negotiate the time of your sentencing down from there. This is just the starting point of our negotiation." My mind shut off after hearing forty-eight years in prison. My life was over when I heard that. Hearing a possible forty-eight years in prison didn't influence me into taking accountability for my actions. In fact, after hearing a possible half-century for my crime and accident, I went the opposite way. I quit. I quit caring about life at that point and frankly gave up. Luckily, a few weeks later my attorney called me with the second round of negotiations, stating that my potential sentence had been narrowed down from the forty-eight years to thirty-six years. The following month, the third negotiation was at twenty-four years in prison. Finally, a few weeks before sentencing, with the negotiations ended, the judge could give me no more than a maximum of ten years in the Department of Corrections. My attorney did a great job, even though I received the longest sentence for a DUI vehicular homicide in my county in the last twenty-five years. Rumors were floating around that the judge was making an example out of me. My ten-year prison sentence and a five-year parole sentence didn't scare me into accountability all of a sudden. It wasn't the moment the judge slammed the gavel down, blurting out my sentence in the courtroom of ten years in prison. It wasn't the first six-to-eight months of twenty-three-hour lockdown and isolation in a cement box hidden from the world that would influence me into accountability.

The moment it all changed for me was when the Department of Corrections bus parked in front of the boot camp building. This building was where I would spend the next eleven-plus months of my incarceration. A light switched on in my brain literally the moment the drill instructors came racing in on the bus, screaming, "You fucking scum, inmate trash, DOC shitbags, you faggot maggots, we are going to destroy you inmate fucks." That singular moment instantly shifted me from an immature boy to a man. My life shifted and my brain began rearranging my circuitry, ultimately making me become a better person. Boot camp was the best thing that could have happened to me at the time. The boot camp was designed to break all inmates down to the lowest of the low in order to rebuild that person back up again. It was designed to take the immature young men who had no accountability for the choices they made up until that point and rearrange their entire perspective on life. Boot camp was successful in building me back up again from the ground up.

The program was only ninety days, and it was created to bring out the best of the inmates using accountability, discipline, integrity, routine, and a list of other force-feed adjectives, all aimed to benefit the inmates (a.k.a. recruits). It was devised to be hardcore to the core. It was intended to be so difficult that if you graduated in ninety days, that's it. In ninety days the judge was likely to reduce your prison sentence. Ninety days and the judge would let you out of prison early to see your friends and family. My platoon started with forty-five recruits on day one, "zero day" as they would call it. By the time the program was over on day ninety, only fourteen recruits, myself included, marched in those graduation lines. Thirty-one young men quit on their friends, family, and potential to get out of prison due to the difficulty of this life-changing program. By not graduating, you were willing to stay incarcerated for the remainder of your prison sentence. Meaning you intentionally chose to stay in prison longer instead of pushing through boot camp rules and regulations. There was no way I was not going to take advantage of this unbelievable opportunity to get out of prison sooner than later. I still had nine years and six months left on my sentence. My hope was to get a couple of years shaved off for graduating.

Every morning TAPS, a military trumpet of respect through musical notes, was blaring through the intercom system just before the lights were to be turned on in the squad bay for the day to begin. The drill instructors would race into the squad bay screaming obscenities and military sayings at the top of their lungs. We would run in place and do hundreds of pushups and sit-ups before even having a chance to brush our teeth. We were under the full control of the drill instructors (DIs). These drill instructors were actual military men, coming from nearly every branch of the military services. One of my boot camp drill instructors was a Green Beret. He was one of the baddest dudes I have ever encountered. On one of the first mornings, he casually told us that he could kill us one hundred different ways with a basic shoestring. Let's just say I was terrified. We had drill instructors from the Marines, the Army, and even the Air Force. The Air Force DI was the easiest on us, but he still had every intention of breaking the inmates down at a moment's notice.

We were only allowed to speak in the classroom or when spoken to by one of the DIs. Our mandatory response would always have to be yelled at the top of our lungs. "Sir, yes, sir. Recruit Fisher requests to attack the head, sir." That was the response for permission to go to the bathroom—if they felt like allowing you to pee. Depending on the DI and the time of the day, they would make you hold it until they felt so inclined to let you relieve yourself. We stood in corners with buckets on our heads. We stood at attention for hours every day, staring at the walls. We were not allowed to move or speak, and if we did either, the entire platoon would get punished with physical exercises. We were accountable not just for ourselves but for every one of our fellow recruits. If one person messed up, spoke, or got caught moving while standing at attention, the entire platoon would be punished. Thirty-one men quit due to a plethora of other boot camp rules, physical trainings, and mental beatdowns the program allowed on its recruits in the ninety days.

The night we graduated from the first thirty-day phase of the program to the second thirty-day phase, we lost a handful of our platoon. The drill instructors had mind games they would play on the inmates. On that night, they had a second serving of dinner planned for us. The naïve recruits who were seeking validation for graduation from the first phase fell right into the trap the DIs had. For the first time in any of our times in prison, we were offered a second serving of spaghetti. We all thought it was some kudos for making it through the arduous physical and mental challenges of phase one. We were wrong. Running carefree to the chow hall line to get our second servings, we were oblivious to the other phases to come and the drill instructors laughing under their breaths. We proceeded to eat our fill, happy as can be. The DIs had a different plan. As soon as we got back to our squad bay, the drill instructors ordered us to drink a full canteen of water. Mind you, this is after eating a second serving of dinner, one our bellies were already not accustomed to. We proceeded to finish our canteens followed by the drill instructors barking out, "To the pit. Take them to the fucking pit. We are about to destroy these pussies!!!!"

The pit was a sandbox where DIs would physically trash recruits with pushups, sit-ups, bear crawls, log rolls, and any other physical exercise the drill instructors could make us do. The DIs proceeded to trash us in the pit for what seemed like hours. By the end of the trashings, twenty-one out of the twenty-six still left in our platoon vomited in the sand pit, where we were bear-crawling, log rolling in each other's vomit and spaghetti noodles. We had our fellow recruits' vomit on our jackets, hats, shirts, and pants. It was disgusting. It was one of the worst nights I've ever experienced.

The discipline, routine, and accountability I learned in boot camp altered the trajectory of my life. It was as if I went from an immature, overconfident, alcoholic asshole to a responsible young man almost instantly. I began valuing the position in life I was in by the choices I made. I could no longer blame others for the predicament I put myself in. The accident had always been my fault; I've never faulted anyone but myself. In boot camp, I began realizing I was accountable for every choice I had made in my life—and not just the choice I made behind the wheel on November 9, 2003. All the schools I failed out of were not my coaches' faults; it was my fault due to the choices I made around alcohol, drugs, and the underlying issues of my mental health. Boot camp was when I began putting all the pieces together to become who I am today. My foundation was being rebuilt. I will forever be grateful for the program that changed my life for the better.

NEW YEAR'S

People, in general, can talk a big game, boasting about their big changes and building themselves up with their inflated self-gloating, social media posts, and profiles. Continuously telling others their grandiose plans involving change and puffing out their chests, they yell out to the world through Instagram or TikTok about how amazing their change will be. There is basically a holiday for that—it's called New Year's. The night of December 31st of any year, you'll hear millions of people say, "Year 202X is going to be the best year of my life. I'm going to change." This must be the most common phrase used around the world the first week of January, until reality starts to sink in and people realize it takes accountability, dedication, and hard work to make that lasting change.

Making New Year's goals and telling the world about your plans is great; it makes you sound ambitious, even important—*but* if you look in the mirror and can't honestly tell yourself you are going to act on your change, plan for your change, and actually follow through on the change, you will continue to struggle like you have been in Part 1 or Part 2 of this book. The reality is ninety-two percent of people who set goals on New Year's Eve don't achieve them.[1] Becoming that eight percent starts with holding yourself accountable to the goals you set. Without accountability, you will get nowhere, and I'm talking about life and not just your New Year's Eve goals.

The biggest accountability goal I've ever set—*never* drink alcohol again! I haven't had a sip since 2004. There have been hundreds of opportunities for me to slip and take just one little drink. There is no chance I will go back to drowning my pain behind a bottle or illegal drugs. That doesn't sound like fun anymore. Besides, I know the dark side of alcohol. I've lost many friendships and relationships to those who don't get that one simple line of accountability on my end. I don't care if somebody twenty-one years or older drinks, but if they offer me a drink, knowing my history or story, then they don't care enough about my life, and I've got no time for their nonsense. They should understand, knowing my path of destruction, and be smart enough to not ask me to drink. If you ask me to drink after knowing my story, you can honestly fuck off. I'm over any semblance of relationships I might have had because of people asking me to drink again. *I have my one line in the sand*, and if you don't like it, sorry—I don't need you in my life. This line in the sand is a perfect example of accountability. I know my limits, I know my issues, and anyone willing to cross that line is no longer in my circle. My circle is small; it might even be too small because I hold others accountable for their actions as well. I've got no time for people who will inhibit my ambitions to dream big and aim for the galaxy. I'm not shooting for the stars, I'm looking to explore space.

ACCOUNTABILITY LADDER

Nothing works unless you are honest with yourself. Be brutally honest with your past, present, and vision for the future. Over the years I've done a quick Google search on images and found some great examples of "accountability ladders." I've personally used different variations of this ladder over the years. In doing so, I'm able to determine where my current state of accountability lies. Many times, it's not where I want it to be. When this takes place, I'm forced into adjusting my own conscious awareness of accountability. The general concept of the varying accountability ladders is that there are rungs of accountability, and you can go both up and down. The ladder starts at the lowest rung, which often is your unconscious behavior and how you navigate life with little to no thought. As you steadily climb each rung, the more aware you become of your choices and the outcomes that follow, increasingly leaving excuses in the dust. The higher you climb the ladder, the more conscious and aware you become. The end goal is to eventually hit the last (or highest) rung. When you fight tooth and nail and finally climb to that last rung, you'll find a sense of peace and accomplishment, knowing you can find solutions to your problems in a accountable way. I've found over the years the more I use this method to determine my own accountably, the better off my life seems to be. It provides a simple formula or visual representation to increase my awareness and perspective about life.

At this point I hope you did a quick web search on accountability ladders and can now honestly evaluate yourself. Where do you stand? Keep in mind you can stand on different rungs based on different situations. Are you still blaming others for your misfortunes? Do you recognize that? If so, what will you do from this very moment to work toward a solution? If you recognize it, have you already made progress toward change and are climbing the next rung on the ladder? How can you make a change? How can you hold yourself accountable for that specific situation that you are thinking about?

Do you own your current station in life? Knowing fair well you made countless decisions to put yourself where you are today. What do you need to change right now to improve your tomorrow?

In my own personal observation of the accountability ladder, one of my biggest challenges has been not finishing this book. Over the past few years, I've begrudgingly posted a handful of social media posts about my book, telling the world I was writing—which I was—and doing a lot of it, but I was doing the New Year's Eve example in my own life. I stopped mentioning my book on social media, realizing it was time to stop saying I was going to finish, no matter the circumstances. I keep asking myself, *Is this the way you want your life to be, failing to finish the book you told others you had in the process*? Would I be just another person who says they are writing a book and never actually does? I can't accept that.

This process has been a grind. So far, I've written over 400,000 words and condensed this book down to 78,000+ words. I could have put out multiple self-published books by now with specific subcategories on Amazon.com that get rankings. Yet when I read some people's self-published books, they have no flow, were probably written in one sitting, contain misplaced words, spelling errors, editing errors, and some are frankly garbage—but these authors *finished* their books. If I look at myself in the mirror, I realize I'm just a hater at this point. Why? Because they did something I have not yet done. Even with my mindset of being a competitor, I can self-evaluate, realizing I have nobody to blame but myself for the delay in my book being published. It's up to me—and only me—to put the words on the page and spend countless hours editing this draft. What I can control is dedicating hundreds of hours of time to this goal, putting in the work, even if I'm not the greatest of writers. I will finish a book without a ghostwriter, holding myself accountable for my work because nobody else can. It's on me to control the time it takes to create the solution, which is the end-product of a book sitting on shelves and nightstands in corporate offices, athletic departments, and prisons. That is the goal, a goal I can strive to reach simply by holding myself accountable to the choice of getting up at three, four, five, or six a.m. and editing. Editing is something I loathe, but it is necessary to produce a quality product. Finishing is solely dependent upon my actions. It's not the actions of the others in my life; they don't help me, they can't help me. I must schedule the time, forcing myself to work toward the end-goal of completion. If there is no progress on my book, I cannot blame anyone else but me.

It's time for you to do the same. Stop blaming others and take accountability for who you are and the moments in life you are in control of. It's up to you. If you hold yourself accountable to the choices you make, life will change. Right now, self-awareness and recognition of your own problems are the beginnings of changing who you are.

CHAPTER 14
KEY 2: C=L

"Easy choices—hard life. Hard choices—easy life."
- JERZY GREGOREK

If I had to sum life up into one word, it would be "choices." Here's my feeble attempt at an equation to look smart. Choices equal life (C=L). A simple math equation. You and I have the power to control our lives based on the choices we make day in and day out. You have the ability, every waking moment of the day, to make choices to change the direction of your life. It's up to you to decide whether to or not. It's completely up to you. There is no denying life will continue to shove, push, and throw uncontrollable moments and situations at you. All I ask is that when those moments or opportunities present themselves, you take some time and analyze as many individual choices as you can think of. Once you honestly assess the choices leading up to that moment, chances are you will discover numerous choices that lead directly up to that situation you are thinking of right now. Seriously consider and think about this. How many simple choices leading up to that moment could have caused that situation to come out entirely different?

THE FIRST EXAMPLE

Did you get in a fight with your significant other? Maybe they said something that got underneath your skin, irritating you and making you mad. Even though they might have made a painful comment, hurting you to the core, there were choices leading up to that moment you could have made to prevent that argument from ever taking place. Rewind to a few hours prior to the argument. Did you make the bed and kiss your partner before you left for work? Did you do something nice for them, like putting the dishes away? Did you help put away the groceries they bought for you? Did you help take the trash out before the argument? Or did you ignore them and not hug them every morning like they deserved, reluctantly showing love and affection to cause this fight? Did you ever think that maybe making one of those choices would prevent your partner from snapping at you because you never help around the house or never treat them right in the morning? You make a few of those nice gestures, and odds are that a fight never takes place, but it's not a one-and-done situation. It requires constant maintenance of thoughtful choices like folding the laundry to help lessen the severity of the struggles you will face. It's a choice that you make, nothing more, nothing less. A simple choice you will decide to make or not to make. That simple choice can lead to a greater, stronger relationship or weaken the bond and slowly destroy it.

THE SECOND EXAMPLE

Due to an auto accident, traffic has come to a halt. You are late to an important business meeting. Frustrated, you hit the steering wheel, yelling out, "This damn accident is holding up everyone. I'm going to be late for my meeting." You blame the traffic, you blame the drivers in the accident, you blame the police for not arriving at the scene of the accident fast enough to have the roads cleared by the time you come through. You blame everyone but yourself. Instead of blaming everyone else but yourself, reverse your thinking and challenge yourself to analyze all your choices leading up to the traffic jam. Ask yourself these questions:

- Did you hit your snooze button once, twice—heck, did you hit snooze three times, possibly losing twenty-four minutes of extra time to get ready versus the twenty-four minutes of bad sleep?

- Did you get sucked up into the social media vortex, surfing Instagram or LinkedIn for ten minutes when you could have used that extra ten minutes to leave earlier, avoiding that future accident and traffic jam in the first place?

Here's the simple fix. Don't hit the snooze button! Secondly, set your alarm for twenty minutes earlier than normal, that way you don't have to rush in the mornings. By not hitting the snooze button and getting up twenty minutes earlier, you added forty-four minutes to your day (a twenty-minute earlier alarm and not hitting the snooze button three times at eight minutes per snooze at the old alarm time). Those extra forty-four minutes will allow you to calmly handle all the unexpected morning issues you never plan for, like dealing with kids, dealing with dogs, and managing your significant other. Another fix— save your social media scrolling until you get home or have a lunch break. If you didn't scroll aimlessly for ten minutes and left on time, you might have avoided the accident in the first place. These are simple and basic choices that alter your day, and by consistently altering your day in a calmer matter, it will do the same to your months, years, and life in general.

THE UNINTENDED CONSEQUENCES OF MY CHOICES

Originally, this part of the book was about the choices I made leading up to the night of the accident. I changed this section to reflect on my current and ongoing situation of my divorce. I figured it was more

relevant to talk about the choices I've made or was making in my relationship, since all too commonly, half of all marriages end in divorce.
The choices I made during the pandemic ruined my marriage. I did
everything I could to keep my business going. I remained vigilant in
my sobriety. I'm proud of keeping my speaking career going and staying sober. What I'm not proud of is the unintended consequences of
my choices during my severe depression that forced me into this pit of
despair, ignoring my wife. Looking back, I could have made so many
different choices to prevent our marriage from failing and falling apart.

At the time of this section being written, I find myself sitting at
the back of a random public library moments after digging for clean
shirts to take on my upcoming speaking road trip. I mention digging
for clean clothes not because I'm living in my car but because my wife
asked for divorce, forcing me to move out of our home with no place
to go. Since that moment, I've been living in Airbnbs, hotels, and my
friend's house, living out of suitcases for over a month and using only
what I needed judiciously. Tomorrow, I head to Arizona, then Texas
and Louisiana, for a total of eighteen days. What really sucks is when I
come back in eighteen days, I'll have no place to go, and it's the reason
why I'm writing the next section. I'm writing about and contemplating
my next gigantic choice in my life, taking you, the reader, along for the
unwanted journey. This is the hardest, most pivotal moment in my life,
after the choice to live or die after the accident.

Here are my big choices to make:

Do I stay in Denver and rent a property with the hopes of reconciliation with my wife? This is what I want to do, even if I have a one
percent chance of fixing our marriage. I will sacrifice by living in some
crappy duplex/triplex or house that allows three dogs and a felon.
The dogs and being a felon baggage instantly cut down my options by
eighty to ninety percent, and one of those reasons was an unintended
consequence of my actions from 2003. I'll throw away money on rent
every month to have my dogs with me and the slightest possibility of
just seeing my wife, even if over a cup of coffee. I haven't seen her or

heard her voice in months now. I'm dying inside, yet I don't think it has even mattered to her.

Do I flee the state, move to a beach, and start my life over? Deep down, my free-life thinking alter ego believes this is the best option for my future. It's possible in a year down the road that I can buy a small house near the beach in Galveston or Corpus Christi (prices are half of what Denver housing is) and begin a new path in my life. My immature, fuck-the-world attitude that I've been fighting against every day is winning the battle as I attempt to pin those thoughts further and further back to be closer to my wife and this marriage. To me, this has been a major sign of growth because I'm fighting the voice saying, *Run, Ethan. Start over. Live the life you dreamed about.* That's true; it was the life I dreamed about and wanted before I met my wife. I did a piss-poor job of conveying to her that I would give up those dreams for her in a heartbeat. It's not her fault because I brought them up over the years, so she truly believed I wanted this traveling life instead of her. I failed to convey the right messaging, which was a factor in why I'm in this lonely library on the precipice of a major life decision. From a speaking and building my real estate portfolio standpoint, running is a smart idea, but one I don't want to do it anymore.

Do I move to San Diego and start my life with one of my best friends? Nate was my roommate/teammate at JWU. Nate was the only person and teammate who offered me a place to stay when I couldn't find apartments in the Denver area because of my felony. We lived together in a small two-bedroom apartment with his baby momma and newborn son. Out of all my friends in this world who have come and gone, he and I stay in contact more consistently than anyone else. Nate and I always dreamed of building a gym and basketball business together. Maybe it's time to build that dream.

Financially, moving to San Diego is a really bad idea. It's more expensive than Denver, and it's very unlikely that I can find a place where I can take my dogs—which is another major decision in my life. I miss my dogs, my best friends. They are my favorite living and breathing things (outside of my ex-wife). But trying to rent a property and travel with three dogs is more than challenging, let alone finding a place for a felon. In doing research before the moves, I've already looked at hundreds of rentals in Denver, Galveston, Corpus Christi, and San Diego. Over half of them will not allow a felon, another thirty to forty percent will not allow one dog, let alone three. I haven't rented a house or apartment in over ten years. I've owned my last two properties, and now I'm homeless with not enough money to buy a house in Denver or San Diego. I'm fucked as of right now.

During this saddening time and process, I've been implementing my five keys and following my own advice. I'm living proof that the five keys are keeping me from self-destructing. Praying in my car, homeless, yet understanding I made choices that put me here, that separated my wife from me, I can only hold myself accountable for this moment in my life. If my five keys helped me stay sober and kept my speaking career going during the pandemic, they will help me through a separation/divorce and the most significant crossroads of choices in my life. I truly believe these five keys can help you, the reader, if you apply them daily and believe in them like I do.

CALL TO ACTION

CHOICES IN REFLECTIONS

Take a moment to reflect on who you are and the life you have created for yourself. Play the CliffsNotes version of your life in your mind while asking these questions:

- What is your earliest memory? How and where did you grow up?

- Where did you go to school, what struggles did you face in school, and what choices did you make around those struggles? Did you not prepare for your ACT or SATs because you were spending time with the person you were dating and did horribly on the tests, preventing you from getting into your top three to five schools you applied for because your scores were lower than needed?

- Were there moments when you could have made different choices that would alter the outcomes and the struggles you've faced?

- Did you battle depression and fail to realize you made a choice to self-medicate versus getting professional help?

- What did you learn from those choices and how are you applying them now? What path are you currently taking? How will you get there? What's your plan of action? What choice will you make after reading this book? Will you take accountability for yourself and the choices you make, or will you continue to blame others for the life you are leading? It's up to you, based on the decisions you make following the completion of reading this book.

- Think about some positive moments in your life that were created due to the choices you made. Did you have the guts to ask out your future husband or wife on a date?

- Did you apply for the job you really wanted and get it?

- Did you have your first-born child and your life changed for the better?

- Feel that smile you just gave yourself while thinking of those great moments. How does it feel? Awesome, right?

From this very second, you can change your thinking. You can start weighing the consequences and outcomes of your future based on the choices you make at this very moment. You can change your life! If I can change my life, you can too. *It's up to you* and only you from this moment in time on.

My hope is you are motivated and inspired by my story after reading all that I've overcome. That you start consciously making choices to change your life. I want to inspire you to start a new job, start your own business, spend more time with your loved ones—all of these would be awesome. You can be inspired, thinking about every choice you make—right now—ultimately changing the direction of *your* entire future! This is a choice you are making at this moment. A choice that is influenced by you and only you. What choice will you make when you are done reading this book?

You have the power to choose. You have the power to change. It's up to you and only you! C=L.

CHAPTER 15
KEY 3: WRITE 'EM DOWN

"By recording your dreams and goals on paper, you set in motion
the process of becoming the person you most want to be.
Put your future in good hands—your own."
- MARK VICTOR HANSEN

It's as simple as this—setting goals and writing them down is a crucial key to living a better life. Without goals, there is no direction or endpoint to focus on and aim for. According to a Harvard study, eighty-four percent of the population have no goals in their lives.[1] They live and walk on this planet, surviving day to day, versus having the desire and ambition to thrive. It's highly likely they are unsatisfied with their lives. According to Gallup's World Poll (citation below), the vast majority of full-time employees in the world dislike their job. Only fifteen percent of the world's one billion full-time workers are engaged at work. The situation doubles in the U.S. but is still a staggering thirty percent engaged. But this still means that roughly seventy percent of American workers aren't engaged and don't like their bosses.[2] They complain about their jobs, they complain about their situations in life, yet do nothing about it. These individuals work a typical 9–5 job from Monday through Friday and are excited for Friday to come (TGIF).

They are excited about the weekends to get away from the misery of their lives and the work week. We spend roughly one-third of our adult lives working, and when you despise your adult job, chances are high that you will be unsatisfied with your life. Those who are unsatisfied will often battle depression and emptiness. They end up discouraged about their lives, yet they won't seek help. They know they don't like their current life and don't know how they can get out of this horrible "Groundhog's Day" life they lead. They are too broke to find another job and are stuck in a vicious cycle of living paycheck to paycheck. Instead of talking to a counselor, they self-medicate, drink, smoke, or use prescription pills to forget the work week. This can and often starts a snowball effect of anxiety and depression from the depressant effects of alcohol and drugs they are consuming. The more they drink, the more depressed they get. It's an ongoing battle that takes millions to the depths of darkness and depression that awaits from the emptiness they feel inside.

Only thirteen percent of the population, according to the same Harvard study, think about their goals. People are ten times more likely to achieve their goals just by thinking about them. Let me repeat that: just by thinking of your goals, you are ten times more likely to achieve them, which seems simple. These are the individuals who have dreams of starting a business, thoughts of getting a new job, and thoughts about saving money for their first chance to buy a home. They know there is more to life than the current situation they are in. Many just don't know how or where to start this new life, but the great thing is they are contemplating the change. This is where *choice* comes into play. It starts with one single choice to take a leap of faith. It starts with one choice to research "how to start a business" or fill out one new job application. It starts with one choice to start a home purchasing fund by putting a few bucks into a house savings account. They might want to go to college or trade school but haven't taken the leap. Again, it starts with one simple choice to research the schools near their residence. It doesn't take much to start, just a choice to do so. It's important to realize that you are more likely to achieve your goals when you think about them. So think about your goals. But if you want to really succeed at them, *write* them down.

That same Harvard study reports that only three percent of the population write down their goals. Those three percent who write down their goals are thirty times more likely to achieve them. There is scientific evidence and proof that if you write down your goals, the neural pathways in your brain expand, creating new processes of thoughts about ways to accomplish those goals because you literally write them down and see them. We always hear about the one percent, which are the richest people in the world. It is very likely that the one percent (unless they were lucky and born into wealth) write down their goals and go after them like a hungry lion. That's the difference between wishing for success and going after success. What would you do if you were thirty times more likely to win the lottery if you were told to write down your winning lotto numbers every day? Would you write them down every day, knowing your likelihood of winning is thirty times more? Of course you would. So why don't you write down your hopes and dreams now?

In my office, I have five goal boards. One goal board contains my daily goals, such as: push-ups, sit-ups, meditations, reflections, journals, and workouts I want to complete every day. Another goal board has my weekly goals, another has my monthly goals, another board has my one-to-three-year goals, and the last board has goals for the next twenty to twenty-five years of my life—these are my big audacious goals. They are written down in places where I can see them every day, and I try to figure out how I will get to those gigantic goals by the time I leave this earth. I don't always achieve my daily, weekly, monthly, or one-to-three-year goals, but my aim and focus is on my long-term, big, audacious goals, which keeps me focused when I fail to accomplish some of my shorter goals. When I have an end-goal in sight, my path toward it might change, but the end is always the objective. It keeps me focused on the big picture, and I don't get frustrated by failing at my smaller goals. Goal setting is one of the most important aspects in life to me. Science has proven it works on the mind and shows how you can accomplish objectives, dreams, and desires.

WHERE GOAL SETTING STARTED

A loud buzz sounds just before the large, thick steel doors are opened. The corrections officer sitting in the control booth controls the movement of the inmates. At this stop, they only open up the doors once for breakfast, once for lunch, once for dinner, and once for an hour of open time. The inmates are in lockdown in those cells twenty-three hours per day.

For me, my only goal was to survive prison. As a first-timer, prison was terrifying. When outside of my cell, I tried my hardest not to show any fear. Fear in prison gives off a scent of weakness; the men in prison take advantage of the weak. I was not going to be one of the weak. I could have been one of them if the situations had been different, but I was extremely fortunate for the prison experience I had. I was blessed and lucky to make it unscathed through those prison fences. Many were not as fortunate as me. At one of the lowest points in my life, locked inside white brick walls, with a very small three-to-four-inch-wide window, and a steel sink, toilet, and mirror combination, I began writing my goals down. Isolation and lockdown force individuals to change—I had to change, I wanted to change. I no longer had any support from coaches, teammates, friends, or family. Alone and isolated, prison was now my home.

I was locked up in those cells for twenty-three hours a day with no TV for the first six months of my incarceration, and there was very little communication for days at a time. It was scary, it was lonely, and again, it was terrifying. Not knowing a single thing about prison life worried me. Who could I talk to, who could I trust, what were the unwritten rules to survive? It was an environment that will change a person; it changed me.

The Denver Rehabilitation and Diagnostic Center (DRDC) is a maximum-security prison, meaning it harbors the worst-of-the-worst. Every incoming inmate is poked, prodded, and psychologically evaluated to determine the level of security prison they would be shipped off to. Upon entering the nightmare of lockdown and isolation, it's a humbling, humiliating feeling when your dignity and every bit of humanity are stripped from you, as well as every article of clothing. Imagine having every inch of flesh and tiny crevice in and on your body examined with the beady eyes of a correctional officer staring at your naked body. They would look deep inside every one of your orifices. It's degrading, it's humiliating, yet there is not much you can do. Your options in prison are to quit caring about life, join a gang, or isolate from everyone. I chose to isolate. I chose to write down my thoughts, my ambitions, and my goals.

Once you enter the fences, you become property of the DOC. You are now an inmate with a number, owned by a gigantic bureaucracy with corrections officers in uniform running the show. The officers often have a major authoritarian complex, trying to show intimidation, and receiving very little respect from the inmates—but they held the power. It's a bizarre power dynamic.

Wearing a DOC number indicates your lowly position in life… an inmate. You are nothing but a dirty, slimy sardine in a sardine can. Nothing more, nothing less. You are a number, not a person. And the longer the DOC number you have, the newer or fresher you were to the system. You were called a newbie, fresh fish, a new cat, or a new number. Those six numbers adorned every article of clothing I owned, minus my socks. It was as if the numbers were tattooed on me. Those six numbers became my identity.

How would I liberate my mind among the endless hours of the day? Sitting, pacing, sleeping in those cells, I made a choice, a choice to better myself. It began by reading every book I could get my hands on, no matter the content. I devoured every page, hustling to finish each book so I could trade it out for a new one. Slowly, my mind began to change. A new level of appreciation for books and other people's stories began taking shape. My self-awareness increased to levels I'd never experienced before, molding my malleable mind and impacting my days of isolation. A new version of me was forming. A new devotion to living was taking over. It didn't stop with books. All inmates were given a red pencil with a lined yellow notepad. This combination became my best friend as I'd write down my thoughts and my goals for hours at a time. It was cathartic, writing out my thoughts, my reflections on the past, and my ambitions for the future. It was a release, a therapy flowing through the red pencil lead. Little did I know at the time, I was addressing my mental health. It was an unexpected benefit with values added to my daily existence in incarceration. Aside from the mental health aspect, I decided to have physical goals every day. I began doing as many push-ups, crunches, burpees, and sit-ups as I could each day in my cell, trying to challenge myself mentally and physically to stay engaged and fit for my chance at the military boot camp. Clarity and drive were forming as the red pencil charted out my thoughts on the yellow pages about my past, about my future. Questions of who I was and where I was going entered my mind. I began the process of goal setting.

At some point in isolation, my mind was made up—no matter how messed up my prison time was going to be, or how long I was going to be locked up, I made a commitment in my solitary cell to be the best man possible. I made a choice to work as hard as I could at everything. What was presented was a unique opportunity in front of me. It was all about perspective, and my perspective was to turn this horrible rock bottom into something positive. Even though I was in a cell and deserved to be in a cell, I was alive. I was breathing. I was ambitious, I was driven, and I began writing down my goals. My first major goal included a promise to God to not let Bill (the man who lost his life to my drunk driving decision) and his family down—even if they never wanted me to see the light of day again. It was time to become a new man, a new version of myself for what I thought would be the next ten years of my life in those brick walls. An inner voice kept saying, *Push harder, be better. No matter what's in front of you, handle it with determination. Fucking change.* Little did I know that I was not only creating and setting goals each day for my workouts but I was beginning to create long-term goals and ideas as I wrote them down. This was a first for me, as I've mentioned numerous times in this book. Before the accident, the only goals I had were to play basketball, get drunk, do drugs, and maybe get laid if I was lucky. In what I called my past life, there were never any goals, just outrageous delusions and far-out dreams.

I began writing "when I get released" goals. The getting-out goals were my motivation. They were exciting, energetic, powerful, and thrilling new goals I had never had prior. A new energy in my life was taking shape. These goals began forming on the yellow pad, and something began to change as I read them over and over and saw them every day. I was believing in what I was writing down. Every goal I wrote down was something I wanted to attack and push toward. I began having something I'd never had before, and it was *hope*. Hope was created by writing down my goals. The numerous notebooks and notepads with hundreds of pages of written concepts, ideas, poems, and rhymes helped my sanity. I would go to the library at every opportunity that I had. At my second-to-last prison location, I went to the library nearly every day to educate myself toward the freedom goals I was writing in my cells. You could find me reading every single edition of *Entrepreneurship* magazine, every business or marketing book that was on the shelves in the Rifle Branch Library. Any piece of knowledge I could gather would walk back with me to my prison cell. In my cell, I would begin writing down what I learned, what I needed to start companies, and how I was going to get to these audacious goals.

I had no idea that these prison habits and routines would later become keys to future success. It's hilarious to think you are taking advice to change your life from a man who unknowingly began using these five keys behind the barbwire fences of low-security prisons. These keys didn't exist on paper until I was creating a keynote speech and workshop for the inmates at Florence Federal Prison in 2017. In crafting the speech for the men there, I began going through the notebooks I wrote in during my three years in prison. I found a page dated 9/15/06 in my Business Plan Notebook titled "Released," and it listed out a plan to help inmates better their lives. I had no idea that I wrote down "prison talks" until one of the inmates at Florence pointed it out. He said, "You literally wrote down 'speaking to inmates,' and here you are, speaking to inmates," and the entire room went silent—they were all in awe. Without my prior knowledge and intention, they could now fully grasp and understand the power of writing down your ambitions, dreams, and goals. They had proof from the goals I had written down nearly eleven years prior to that event that goals do come true if you write them down and go after them.

At that time in 2006, I had zero intention of being a keynote speaker. As a matter of fact, I didn't even know what a keynote speaker was until 2011 when I saw my first speaker in person. It changed my entire life. After seeing that speaker tell his story, I made a choice that day that I would do what he did, but with my story. I haven't looked back since.

CALL TO ACTION

Begin writing down and charting your goals.
List specific goals in each of these sections:

- Daily goals: What do you want to achieve each day to be better, to self-improve? Is it health, family, mind, or a combination of all? This can be as simple as saying, "I love you" once a day to your loved ones or reading, praying, or meditating for five minutes per day.

- Weekly goals: Objectives that need to be done within the week— paying bills, saving money, finishing a project.

- Monthly: These are bigger goals, possibly planning for a larger achievement—investing $100 dollars into a real estate investment fund for your first home or rental property.

- Six months: A lot can be achieved in six months if you dedicate time, effort, resources, and schedule appropriately. What do you want to accomplish in six months? Starting a side hustle? Starting a legitimate business? Taking a vacation?

- One year: Who do you want to be in a year? Do you want to have saved ten to fifteen percent of a down payment for a new home? Go on vacation with your loved ones? Start a new business and be hiring your first employee? Give yourself a date, a goal, and put it where you can see it every day. So you can chase that year-long goal every day.

Remember to think big, dream big:

- Five years: This is a much bigger goal. Are you starting a family? Buying that new home? Getting out of credit card debt? Traveling the world?

- Ten years: This is a big, audacious goal. Do you want to have multiple income-generating properties? A new career? Your own thriving business? If so, how big is your business? Where will it be? How much is it generating in revenue or how many people are using your product or service?

- Twenty years: Retirement plans. For all of you younger individuals reading this, if you plan retirement and take care of your finances now, you can have a financial security blanket, creating the life you want at forty or fifty years of age if you plan now. Do you want to travel the world? Live in a travel destination?

CHAPTER 16

KEY 4: PERSEVERANCE— BEND BUT DON'T BREAK

"Most people fail, not because of lack of desire,
but because of lack of commitment."
– VINCE LOMBARDI

If it wasn't for God and a round leather ball that bounces, I haven't the slightest clue of where I would be today. My first thought…dead.

Battling the invisible demons of anxiety, depression, and constant suicidal ideation led to my visible war with alcoholism and substance abuse. More than likely, I was on a path toward an early grave. Like I've mentioned before in this book, I wanted to die most nights from eighth grade until the accident at twenty-three years old. It's strange how I don't recall having thoughts of suicide during prison, at the halfway house, or during my time at JWU working on all my degrees. Why was this? Frankly, I was too busy trying to survive and beat the prison system to think about suicide when I was locked away behind those razor wire fences. Once released, I was having too much fun to even consider wanting to die during my time as student athlete. Being out of prison and having the blessing of playing college basketball again, going to school, and being sober made me elated. I was happy to be in school, I was happy to be playing ball, and I was fulfilled working nearly every hour of every day, seven days per week. My twenty-plus hour days of schoolwork, basketball responsibilities, and work for my father's company fulfilled my life.

The times when I struggle are when I have idle time on my hands, as the famous quote "Idle hands are the devil's playground" goes. The entire pandemic was idle time, even though I was working sixty hours per week trying desperately to keep my speaking career alive. The work I was doing was boring and mundane, and frankly, I hated it. The work was necessary to keep my speaking career going, but I dreaded every day of my life during the pandemic. It ruined my life and marriage. I can't blame the pandemic because I had choices every day to change my life and my marriage. Even though the pandemic was harder on me than prison, I had no excuse not to fill my time with books, classes, games, and a loving relationship. I shut down because my career was shut down. I had put all my energy and emotions into speaking and was destroyed when I lost it. Speaking is not just a paycheck or business to me. It's the sole reason I believe I'm still alive. It's my purpose in life. Now that I'm back on stage and speaking, my excitement toward life has returned. It's a blessing to work and do what I love again after such a long hiatus. The pandemic nearly ended my speaking career, but just like my basketball story, I was not going to let something beat me. I might bend, but I won't break.

My life exemplifies *perseverance*, and I can write this with confidence because I know how hard it was to get to where I am today. It's unlikely many in my shoes would have kept pushing forward toward their goals like I have done. Much of the population would have quit a long time ago, never making it to this point I am currently at.

Perseverance wasn't just after the accident. I believe I was born with it. It's the "it" that flows in my veins, somewhere deep in my DNA structure, growing stronger over time. I came out of the womb ready to fight. Before I took my first breath, I was already facing difficulties, being born with jaundice due to being born in the highest elevation hospital in the lower forty-eight states. My body was born into an abnormal atmospheric pressure. Life near 10,000 feet elevation is a struggle for most, especially a newborn baby. My little lungs and organs struggled. They battled and fought to keep me alive. Perseverance flowed in my veins in middle school when all I heard was "You are too small to play" for every sports team. It flowed in my veins when I made the high school basketball team as a five-foot-five, 135-pound sophomore, and by my junior year, starting varsity for a Top 10 team in the state. The doubters and naysayers said I'd never play at that level. The doubters and naysayers said I would never play college basketball; I was too small. I would compete to prove them all wrong.

The breakdown: about three to five percent of nearly 600,000 seniors across the country who play varsity basketball in high school will ever get a chance to play college basketball at the NCAA level, and it's even harder in today's world with the new NCAA transfer portal for graduating high school players trying to play in college. College coaches are recruiting transfer portal players and not graduating high school players like they did in the past. Roughly four to seven percent will play on scholarship at one of these levels of college basketball, ranging from the most well-known Division I schools down to your lesser-known Division II, Division III, junior college, and National Association of Intercollegiate Athletics (NAIA) institutions. To be a college athlete, no matter what sport they specialize in, takes an unbelievable amount of work. Many student athletes work their entire youth lives to even have the slightest opportunity to play in college, spending countless hours training, running, working out, competing, and traveling—it all adds up. It takes perseverance through academics, doubters, haters, injuries, and size limitations to make it to that next level from high school to college. Nearly twenty-five percent of all Division I athletes drop out at the end of the first semester each year because of how difficult it is to be an athlete. There are many circumstances that contribute to this high quit rate, such as being away from home, being a first-generation college student, and taking harder classes than the previous high school level. The reality is, while the athlete might have been the best at their high school, the best in their conference, or even in their respective state, they're going to show up at pre-season training to compete against others that were the best in their school, conference, and state. The athlete soon realizes that they can't compete at that level, and they quit. They quit on their dreams and all that they worked for and overcame because of their circumstances. It's sad but very common. How many athletes that quit their first year go back and try again, maybe at a smaller school or closer to home? Not many. I believe it's much easier to find another opportunity or a second school to play at if they were recruited before—if the athlete is willing to put in the time and effort and didn't burn any bridges at their previous school. The reality is, only a handful go on to try a second school, even if it's at a lower level of competition. Those twenty-five percent who quit as a first-time college athletes give up because it was too hard the first time, and rarely do they go for a second try, much like one-time entrepreneurs who quit the first time they fail and seldom go back.

In my five keys keynote, I briefly discuss the persistence of Bill Gates (even though he has been in some hot water socially), Thomas Edison, Oprah Winfrey, and Howard Schultz of Starbucks. Each one of these incredibly successful individuals faced countless roadblocks and obstacles yet found ways to persevere through it all to become who they currently are. Take the Bill Gates situation: when he was starting Microsoft, it has been said that he pitched the business plan to 1,200 potential investors. Nine hundred said no, three hundred signed up, and only thirty-five were serious about being a part of Microsoft. In the end, eleven made Bill Gates and Microsoft one of the richest men and companies on the planet. My question to all the readers is: How many of you are willing to hear *no* nine hundred times to your dreams like Bill Gates did? Not many, I can safely assume. Most will hear the word *no* once and quit on their dreams. Take the story of Thomas Edison. He failed upwards of ten thousand times at creating the light bulb, yet he never stopped pursuing his vision, his dream, and his purpose. Again, how many people reading this book are willing to fail over ten thousand times at their dreams?

I was willing to fail in order to chase my goal of finishing my basketball career. My basketball story highlights the sheer will and determination through unwavering perseverance, which is what it takes not to quit on a dream, on a goal. How many athletes are willing to try a third school, how about a fourth school, or how about a fifth school? Even more unlikely, how about a grand total of six attempts? Honestly, I can't find that data because it is very unlikely to exist. If you come across somebody who went to six college basketball programs over a ten-year period like I did, please connect me with them, as I would love to talk about our hoop/sports life together—we might even be able to write a book or do a podcast together. Let's shrink the percentages even lower, considering my legal circumstances. How many people can say they created six college opportunities over a ten-year period, finishing up their college basketball career as a twenty-eight to thirty-one-year-old playing with a bunch of eighteen to twenty-one-year-old college students? Seriously, what are the odds that this five-time college basketball failure would find a sixth school at the old age of twenty-eight wearing an ankle monitor? Yep, that's correct. When playing for my sixth school, I was property of the Colorado Department of Corrections. I literally found the only college on the planet I could play basketball at due to my DOC legal parameters. This is the most basic odds of my chance to play again (one in 1,300 four-year universities equals 0.0008 percent), and JWU-Denver was literally the only college out of a total of 1,300 four-year institutions I could play at. I couldn't play at any junior or community college due to my playing eligibility being used up.

It would have been damn near easier to start my life over, stay sober, and work toward making it to the NBA. Only 0.03 percent of high school basketball players make it to the NBA, and I'll admit I'd never play in the NBA, even if I made all the right choices in the world. I truly believe I'm the only person on the planet who did what I did from a basketball standpoint, let alone play and excel, considering I could only play in home games. I was not allowed to leave the Denver metro area for away games. But I started in every home game, and in doing so, earned all-conference and the MVP award for our conference tournament. Luckily, the tournament was at home. The numbers are staggering—it was a once-in-a-lifetime opportunity that I took full advantage of, all while heavily struggling and gripping with the process of recovering mentally from committing a DUI vehicular homicide while playing college basketball with an ankle monitor and parole officers showing up unannounced at my home games, practices, and at my apartment. They were looking for any possible action I would take to send me back to prison for the remainder of my DOC sentence. Mentally, I was still destroyed inside about taking an innocent man's life. That was and is still significantly harder to live with than any preseason conditioning, basketball game, or finals project. The basketball was easy; it was persevering through the eleven total years in the Department of Corrections system, recovering mentally from the accident, going to school, and dealing with life that caused the most trials and tribulations. Basketball was the bonus—it was the cherry on top. Playing college basketball again was a goal I had written down in prison, and I achieved it. I literally did something that had never been done before—playing college basketball as property of the Department of Corrections in Colorado. All because I had goals and I chanced them and was willing to persevere through any roadblock in my way to make my goals happen.

I know what it's like to battle, fight tooth and nail for some goal in my life. I know what it's like to fight each day for the things that I love, enjoy, and want to achieve. My question to you, the reader, is: What do you love this much that you would face as many roadblocks and obstacles as I did, all in order to play a game that you didn't even get paid to play? Can you find something inside of you that is willing to fight, sacrifice, and push for like I did?

WHAT IS INSIDE OF YOU?

No matter who you are, whatever your goals are in life, you must find a spark to overcome unforeseeable moments to achieve what you want in this life. To achieve spectacular accomplishments, an individual must sacrifice significant moments to reach the desired outcome. It takes uncommon strength and total commitment to one's desires to chase a dream. Never letting up and continuing to endure for no specific amount of time, as some goals might never happen. It takes a level of intestinal fortitude that very few have to see their goals all the way through.

Prior to late 2011, becoming a motivational speaker was never a goal. I never imagined or even wanted to be featured in a *New York Times* Best Sellers leadership book, interviewed on HLN/CNN, or placed on numerous speaking bureaus. It wasn't until I saw Mark Sterner speak at JWU in 2011. After his captivating university keynote speech and program, I knew what I wanted to do with my life. I made a choice at that moment to do what he did from the stage—I was enamored by his ability to change lives. Witnessing his program was a monumental pivot in my life. Taking a leap of faith, I made a choice to chase a vision I saw. There would be countless roadblocks and obstacles attempting to prevent me from obtaining the goals I created. This has been more difficult than any of my attempts at playing college basketball. I love my career and purpose, but the business side wears me out. I've been close to resigning from this arduous task as a speaker, yet I do as the chapter heading says, "Bend but Don't Break."

Life is trying and taxing no matter how many good choices you make. When chasing your goals, you will face what seems to be insurmountable hindrances and burdens in your quest for success. Are you willing to be broke and lose all sources of income to chase your business dream like I've done the last decade, especially during the pandemic? Are you willing to sacrifice friendships, relationships, and any stability to chase these dreams? Do you have enough confidence and tools in your toolbox to chase the big, audacious dreams you have, fully aware that hard times are likely to follow? Are you willingly ready to get punched in the gut by the force of Mike Tyson, standing there knowing it's what you must do to achieve greatness? No matter how many good choices you make, life will always hit you with unexpected roadblocks. What drive do you have inside to persevere and withstand the hurricanes and storms in life?

Please learn from my failures. Prior to 2004, I wasn't willing to sacrifice my life, or fun, for the game I loved. Now I am because I have a second chance at life. A new story to write. I've proved to others and myself that I'm willing to sacrifice to achieve success. I have no social life. I have no friends. Before the pandemic, I was living in a pandemic-like world. I haven't golfed, gone on vacations, or taken more than a few days off in a row from working in years. I work every day, some days more than others, but every day I'm planning, thinking, visualizing, writing, dealing with emails, or researching for my businesses. I rarely get paid for all the work behind the scenes—all of my efforts go into a paid speech. Almost everything I do is work-related. People tell me all the time I need a work/life balance, but when you are passionate about a career, passionate about your life purpose, driven to helping others, speaking is not work to me. What consists of work is trying to find speaking events, sitting at a computer going on weeks and even months straight in the beginning years, without any speeches booked. That is taxing. That is work, and it's tough, but I always know it will pay off eventually, and it has. I've spoken at over 500 events, and that number is growing quickly. No matter the complications and snags in my way, I will persevere. I was born of adversity and am willing to sacrifice to achieve what I deem to be "success." Are you?

CALL TO ACTION

This is a big challenge.

I challenge you to chase your dreams.

- You must persevere through the challenging times to achieve your dreams, your passions, your purpose, and what you love in this world.

- Dedicate yourself to be who you want to be in life, not who else somebody wants you to be.

- Commit yourself to being the best student you can be, the best athlete you can be, the best entrepreneur you can be, the best partner, or the best parent you can be.

- Sacrifice the things you truly don't desire and focus on *you* and your life. Sacrifice for the sanctity of marriage, the love of your kids, and the pursuit of happiness. Sacrifice for the things you love, sacrifice for your passions, sacrifice for your purpose, and learn to take accountability for your faults.

- Bend but don't break in your quest for success.

CHAPTER 17
KEY 5: FAITH

"We all must have faith in something. Without faith, there is no hope."

– MARK MANSON

It does not matter if you are an atheist, pray to Allah, meditate on Buddha, believe in Catholicism, sing for Jesus, identify as Jewish, or go to a church for some religion I've never heard of. It doesn't even matter if you consider yourself spiritual like I do. Heck, it can be none of the above. You can believe in one, none, or all of these beliefs and still have *faith*. Faith will keep you going in the darkest of times. It's helped me through the accident, prison, college, the pandemic, and now divorce. Faith is the complete trust in something. It's having faith in yourself, faith in the choices you make, and faith in your purpose in life. Once I found faith, my life completely changed. My intention and hope in these pages are to help you become aware that faith will lead you to your purpose. Faith will lead to your success and what you are seeking. Understand that faith is not a one-and-done objective. It takes constant maintenance. Your faith will be challenged—it will be tested for you to maintain.

Unequivocally, one hundred percent, I am who I am today because of God. Take it for what you want; I'm not here to influence you or any others into my spiritual beliefs. I'm not a fan of organized religion. I don't go to church, but I pray every day. I talk to God every day. I am the man I am today because of my faith in God and faith in my purpose in being alive. I believe there is something much greater than me, greater than you or any other human on this planet out there. Before the accident, I had no belief in a higher power. I always felt like there was something out there—but what, I had no clue.

Everything in my life changed on November 9, 2003. The tragic night of the accident. Waking up from a blackout and the nurse telling me, "You killed somebody," upended everything; my life was flipped upside down. Uncontrollable tears fell for hours, and at some point, the tears slowed, leaving me in a dark hospital bed replaying those words over and over in my head. *You killed somebody. You killed somebody.* It was a nightmare that wouldn't stop, and my reality began to sink in. Running was my first thought—running to a far-off place where nobody could find me. The second was suicide—the quickest way out of this horrible situation. The third option…God. God told me to handle my responsibilities, and from that moment, something changed. Words cannot attempt to describe or explain what I felt. There are no words to say to do it any justice. There were no flashing lights, no powerful beam of light, no voice from the cosmos shaking my hospital room as it echoed into my life. There was no visual stimulus or out-of-body experience followed by a voice like all the movies typically feature. Yet a resounding, powerful understanding that God told me to handle my responsibilities overcame me. It was like a switch was flipped in my brain, opening an energizing faith in what life meant. Clarity came into focus from the cloudy fog of reality that took place only a day before. A resounding energy and belief were all that mattered. It was now time to handle my responsibilities.

Scientists and non-believers might call this critical juncture PTG (post-traumatic growth). It might scientifically be just that, but my understanding and *faith* in what took place is mine and nobody else's. I know exactly how much I've changed my life since that very moment and why I changed. I'm much different, a better version of a human being than I was in 2003, and I'm proud of that. God gave me a second chance.

Over the next few months after the accident, I would face some of the biggest challenges, testing my newly embedded power in faith. An internal fistfight was taking place. The new me versus the old me, the good me versus the bad me. Relying on my newfound belief and faith carried me into a path and direction I was meant to have, yet I had no idea where I was heading at that point in time, except that I had faith that where I was heading was where I was supposed to be. Something internally changed. I was determined to find out what my future was going to be. Even though I knew I was going to prison after the accident, I trusted the path.

PANDEMIC CROSSROADS

There was a time I was surrounded by darkness, devoid of light, figuratively and literally; at one point, locked in cuffs and locked in chains, tormented by suicidal thoughts, alcoholism, drugs, and worst of all, the death of an innocent man. A husband, father, son, and brother is gone from this world due to my choices. For some messed up reason, I'm still breathing. It should have been me who died that night, not Bill. It should have been me that passed to the afterlife. I wish this was the case. I've prayed countless times for that outcome, but the reality is I'm alive and I must attempt to make up for what I did, even though it can never be done.

At times, I feel like a damn cockroach. Whatever the "it" factor is inside of me, it's extremely potent and hard to destroy. Teetering on the edge of collapse countless times, barely treading water long enough to be helped up on shore by some star-crossed sailor, God never let me quit! Even when I wanted to, even when I questioned the reasons for still being here. That complete trust in faith is what keeps me going.

Months into the pandemic, a severe depression hit like an atomic bomb, leaving me in an apocalyptic desert of nothingness, void of life, color, and joy. Drowning in icy water, deep below the earth's surface, in a cave of darkness that has never seen a hint of sunlight, not even a reflection, is where, regrettably, my mind went. Anyone who truly knows me understands I tend to go from lighthearted and jovial to darkness in a matter of moments. Over the years, I've learned ways to take a moment, breathe, and focus on the positive things in my life and the people I won't let down. Then the pandemic shifted that. Something broke inside my mind. I wasn't me—I wasn't the same man who made it through the accident, I wasn't the same ambitious seeker of my future, and I wasn't the man I once was. I reverted to the old childish me—it was destructive. It was so bad that I pushed my wife away in the process. I began taking medication for the first time in nearly seventeen years, hoping that it would help. It only made it worse. They put me on the wrong medications, and I continued to be broken, tormented, and lost, ready to give up on life. Yet, deep down, my faith kept me working toward my goals and dreams. Faith was there in the basement office, keeping me alive, keeping me breathing, when on the surface, I was falling apart. My attention was on my business goals and not my personal goals with my wife, and things dropped faster than the stock market on Black Monday. My wife lost faith in me because I put my faith in my work and not in us. The second biggest regret in my life.

No matter how many good choices you make in this life, there will always be aspects that are uncontrollable. The years 2020–2022 have been a perfect example of that. The global pandemic devastated billions of lives, killing millions of innocent people. The global economy was rattled while countless small businesses no longer had the ability to keep open signs in their windows, losing all customers and failing to stay in operation. Families lost loved ones, people lost jobs, and levels of a new struggle never seen before became the new normal. With the new normal came the increasing dangers of poor mental health, like I discussed in Chapters 1 and 2. All I can say is that 2020–2022 flat-out sucked and were the second to worst two years of my life.

The world had no idea how long the pandemic was going to last, and many, including myself, waited for the clock to strike midnight on December 31st, 2020, thinking it would all just disappear. I was under the false assumption that the New Year's Eve ball drop at midnight would take place and this hellish year of COVID-19 would be over. My fingers were crossed, believing the global pandemic would stop. The pain would finally end, as if a magical switch would shut off at midnight. Boy, was I wrong; the world was wrong. We couldn't have been more wrong. Once the New Year started, I shifted my mindset and assumed the pandemic would last until the summer of 2021. I was wrong again. The isolation, depression, anxiety, and struggle would continue for much longer than most of us could have imagined. January 2021 through August 2021 were the worst for me. Nothing had changed with schools, and I was still on unemployment, scraping to get by, trying to get a few online events here and there, hoping for things to open, yet they never did. That's when things really began to fall apart in my marriage. I was mentally exhausted from working sixty-plus hours per week for no pay. My depression hit its rock bottom, and I began ignoring my wife. My sadness for my lack of work and companies failing carried over into my personal life, destroying the only good thing I had during the pandemic—my wife. It's as if two-plus years were wiped out from the global timeline, as only a small percentage of the world used the lockdown for a launching pad to growth and prosperity.

Does that mean the world has lost all sense of hope? No. Does that mean we lost all sense of drive and passion? No. Being fully transparent as a "motivational or inspirational keynote speaker," it's been an extremely difficult roadblock to remain focused, stay positive, and keep moving forward. The pandemic was one of the toughest obstacles and roadblocks I have ever faced. Yes, I just said that. Living with Bill's death will never go away; that is the harsh reality I must live with, and no period of time will cure it. The only cure will be when I pass from the living to the dead. The pandemic was the second worst time in my life. It ruined my life, and it ruined my marriage.

There were two major choices laid out on the table for me during the pandemic. One, quit my speaking career, get a job, be normal, embrace a 9–5 life. Or, two, plant my feet into the ground, clench my fists, and fight tooth and nail to keep my speaking career going. I didn't want a 9–5 job, and that destroyed my marriage. I had faith every day I would regain my speaking career but lost faith in my marriage along the way. For that, I'm beyond destroyed, as my wife was the best gift I had ever had. I took her for granted, and she lost faith in us. That loss of faith equated to a loss of a love and marriage. Here, I find myself nearly two years removed from living with my wife, now living in an empty house, not knowing anyone in Houston but my dogs. I still miss my wife more than she will ever know. I miss our life, and it's all been lost because I lost faith in us. Faith is not just some religious, spiritual belief. Faith is the trust in the daily things we take for granted. I lost faith in the small things that I had once appreciated before the pandemic. I lost faith in the little amazing things my wife did, and I lost faith in our bond. I lost faith, and I ended up losing her. Therefore, faith is so important. When you believe in something so much, nothing will break it apart. She lost her faith in me, and now we are no more.

FAITH CONTINUES

My hope is this book provides a few little nuggets of strength a reader can take away in a moment of weakness in their respective lives. I'm not perfect! I don't have it all figured out, but like this section of the chapter, I have complete *faith* in my purpose. I have complete *faith* in my "calling" as a preventative, story-telling keynote speaker. *Faith* has me to a point in life where I truly believe, without a shadow of a doubt, in my *why*. I'm alive, I'm breathing for a reason. I hear it all the time, "If you can save one life by speaking, you've done your job." That sounds great, but I'm not satisfied with that. I'm on a mission to change millions of lives. I have faith that I'm supposed to write this book and many others to influence the lives of those I don't have the honor of speaking in front of. Everything I want to do is to change lives and serve others. I have faith in my purpose and faith in my path.

When my life feels like one moment away from a complete meltdown and collapse, I close my eyes, take numerous deep breaths in, and quickly reflect on my life and all I've been through. My thoughts are often about Bill's life, Bill's family, my family, and all the hundreds of millions of people who struggle far worse than you and I. There are days I imagine young kids and adults who can't read this book for lack of education, or those who are born into a kind of poverty nobody reading this book would wish on any other human being—vividly seeing them sleeping on dirt floors, heads near heaps of trash with nasty smells of stagnate sewage water being breathed in with every breath. I just imagine those with no running water, no clean water to drink. I've seen videos and read articles and stories of those in these forsaken situations, yet many smile, laugh, and play with their friends as if their horrid situations don't exist. Their parents raise their kids with joy, as they are all blessed to be alive. My mind visualizes these moments and those who are trapped in a life with no way out. It makes me realize how amazing my life is, and there is no fucking way I should pout about my first-world problems, yet I still do in those moments I lose grip on myself. That is why I close my eyes, breathe, and visualize; it calms me down and allows me to realize I've been given numerous opportunities in life. I've been given an amazing life and career, so even when things are dark and the struggle is all I feel, deep down I know I'm in a good place in this world. Better days will come back if I work at it. Better days will come if I hold myself accountable to my situation and realize I put myself in this moment by the choices I've made. It's up to me and only me to get out of my own way because I have *faith* in why I'm still alive and breathing.

CALL TO ACTION

What do you have the utmost faith in?

- Do you have faith in who you are as a person? Do you have faith in your relationships? If not, how will you change and start creating positive momentum toward the faith you need to be successful?

Write down a handful of goals you have.

- Ask yourself, do you truly believe and have faith that you will achieve them?

If you say no, is it because you don't have a plan to get to those goals?

- If that is the case, go back to goal-setting. Write down your step-by-step process and plan for achieving your goals. Make sure you have small, achievable steps you can accomplish. Why? Every time you accomplish a step toward your goal, it will boost your confidence and your faith that you can and will accomplish those goals.

PART 4

SUCCESS BEGINS WITH A FOUR-LETTER WORD (LOVE)

Part 4 is about self-love, vulnerability, and gratitude. In my opinion, these three emotionally divisive expressions are critical to achieving success. Without love, depression, doubt, and self-loathing are not far away. We need to learn how to love and care for ourselves and for others. It starts by being vulnerable and grateful for the things we have in this life.

Less than a decade ago, I would have laughed and made excessive fun of the current/present me for talking about love and vulnerability. To be forthright and vulgar, I would have called my current self a gigantic "pussy." Following the female genital reference, the next few words likely to follow would be "ass bitch." Yep, I would have called myself a pussy ass bitch. Harsh, sexist, and vulgar words—I know. I'm sorry if I offended you, but that's the truth of what would have come out of my mouth. My mouth can easily be worse than a drunk sailor whose father was abused by an alcoholic, truck-driving father. One of my favorite quotes growing up was "nut up." Another popular one was "Grow a pair," all provided by my favorite basketball team of all time, the "Fab 5" from Michigan. As you can see from the last few sentences, my dirty mouth, anger, and ego are not a healthy mix. Even worse was when I mixed alcohol with the intention of destroying others with a verbal onslaught of obscenities. Somewhere inside the recesses of my cerebral cortex, those words still hover near the tip of my tongue. Have I changed? Heck yeah. Do I still have that old programming? Heck yeah. Yet, I've grown and matured, learning to control my mouth most of the time. Over the years of maturity, I've learned to keep my sailor mouth at bay, fully aware of its possibility to destroy any relationship and burn any bridge I encounter. My maturity has grown because I'm now able to use the "L-word" (love). I'm a different human being now that I've allowed and embraced love in the world.

It is natural to express your feelings. What's not healthy is to cover up your feelings, hiding what you determine to be weaknesses like some CIA, secret Area 51, "new world order" domination plans. As a man, you can still be strong and say, "I love you." You can still be strong and say you "love" life. You can portray yourself as this macho, hardcore, tough man with the vibe that nothing can hurt me and still say "love." You can be a man's man and still say, "I love you." I'm a mean S.O.B. when I want to be. But I've learned how to embrace the internal strength to tell others I love them. It takes balls, it takes self-confidence and strength to tell somebody you love them. It's not a weakness, it's a strength.

A strong man is needed in many situations, yet there is a time and place to express how you feel and show your emotions. Men are typically known for hiding the brunt of their emotions internally, often leading to alcohol use, substance abuse, and numerous mental health issues—hence, middle-aged men being the demographic with the highest suicide rates. Roughly sixty-nine to eighty percent of suicides are men, not women or kids, but *men*, yet we brush it under the rug as if it's no big deal. Millions of men have died from alcohol and suicide. Roughly three-quarters of alcohol-related deaths are by men as well.[1] If we could talk to those men before they died, I'd bet large amounts of money that they were struggling with some emotional event that they needed to talk about but were afraid or embarrassed and chose not to. Instead, they drowned their sorrows in a bottle, and those who hit the lowest depths take their lives. If they were loving enough to themselves to get the help they needed, they might still be here. Instead, they drank themselves to death or took their own lives. Men have been programmed generation after generation not to talk about or even show emotions that are considered weak, and alcohol suicide statistics back this alarming reality up. It's okay to say I love you, it's okay to say I need help. This is for all the men reading this—I love you; I care for your well-being and only want the best for you. Reach out if you are struggling. That's why I talk about this—so you can feel safe.

CHAPTER 18
IT'S NOT EASY

Without *love*, life will likely be a struggle. To achieve your success, no matter what your specific success might look like, you must love who you are. Become vulnerable, become humbled, be open for growth, and be willing to be open for any type of progress to change. All you need is a little love in what you do and to love who you are. If you see growth through Part 3 using the five keys, self-love will be easier to obtain. But if you still struggle to find consistent success, chances are you are lacking in the self-love department.

Love is not just the love you have for the opposite sex or your significant other. Love is not just about you or your offspring. Love is intended for others; love is intended for life. Love is happiness, love is success, and, more importantly, you need to love yourself in order to maintain your success. What I've learned over my four decades is that without loving myself, my foundation will be unstable.

If loving yourself is hard, I understand. I battle with loving myself every day, just like I battle with my mental health every day. If you don't love yourself, Part 5 and "Success" (discussed later in the book) will likely only last for a short amount of time because you will look in the mirror and dislike what you see. That is why "love" and loving yourself is Part 4 because without love, your success will not last—and to be strong enough to love who you are is the greatest success.

SELF-LOVE IS TOUGH LOVE

This chapter has been the most difficult one to write. Openly discussing love is a challenging topic. It's an uncomfortable topic to address in many households, cultures, and societies—let alone openly discuss and talk about it in public and write about it in a book when you, the author, struggle with it as well. If saying the L-word just made you cringe or made your skin crawl in agony, or just plain made you uncomfortable and you think I'm a weak man for talking about this, you've come to the right book and the right chapter. Love carries a stigma much like mental health. It's weak to say "I love you," or it's weak to say you love yourself, especially if you are a man. I'm fully aware that I'm not the only emotionally guarded, emotionally stunted individual running headfirst into a wall of trouble by locking all my emotions deep inside. This is the case for millions of testosterone-filled male populations. Love is a strength when embraced. Yet, men run from love as quick as they can, placing a negative connotation on it.

These words and concepts would have never left my mouth before 2013–2014 or my early to mid-thirties. The idea that an ex-convict, felon, college athlete with past alcohol and substance abuse issues and a decade-plus of a mentality that invited death would say "love" was nonexistent. There were countless days that I never cared about waking up. I dreaded every day, silently singing the hook from Tupac's "If I Die 2nite" or Biggie's "Ready to Die" over and over. Death excited me for years. I wanted to die. There were periods and points in my life when I had a death wish, never thinking I would ever embrace love.

In my experience, self-love has avoided me on and off for much of my lifetime. It's been a difficult trait to find, embrace, and implement into my daily routines. Love is scary, love is difficult, and love is hard to embrace, especially when you've loathed yourself most of your young life like I have. All I know is when I'm loving myself, I feel nearly invincible at life. Without love, I don't think there is lasting success. Here's my latest example of how important self-love is in my world.

I loved who I was from 2008 to mid-2020. Things were going great. Then the pandemic happened, I hit depression, lost sight of who I was, and lost a sense of my purpose. Feeling like an imposter, I lost my way. I lost the love of self, lost the love of my wife along the way. Once I lost the self-love, my world began to unravel. Therefore, love has its own part in this book.

Loving yourself is a part of success. My success always comes easier when I'm loving myself. I know this, yet it evades me if I don't take the necessary steps to maintain it.

Loving and serving others has always been easy for me. My heart cares deeply for others; that has always been the case. My mother has told me this story numerous times. Even as a first grader, my heart cared for others, as I would give my lunch to a less fortunate kid on my bus who had even less than me, considering at the time my family and I were living in a trailer with no money and were broke. Yet, I continued to give the kid on the bus my lunch because I knew he needed it. I'm proud of the kid I was. I'm proud of that love and heart I had at such a young age. To me that was easy, and everyone should do it. But when you're a child, you don't see all the negativity or social barriers in life, you just see each other's hearts and act based on pure intentions and love.

LOVING EVERYTHING BUT SELF

Growing up, love was never a term used for others. As a matter of fact, I don't think I ever said I love you to my parents until the day I got locked up. I loved hoops, I loved my family, I loved alcohol, and I loved partying, but outside of that, saying I loved anyone was never going to happen. After the accident and heading into prison, everything became even more internalized. Nobody was going to crack my "me against the world, I'm a fuck-up" mentality. At the time, I wanted to feel pain, intentionally holding in my anger, my depression, and the hundreds of hurtful emotions I had for the pain I caused Bill and Bill's family. After the accident, the next eight months of my life before I went to prison were full of darkness. I was on massive amounts of medications that were controlling my neurotransmitters, determining what was firing across my synaptic gaps. At one point, I was placed on suicide watch by my doctors, who were obviously worried about my mental state. They had me on 800mg of the anti-psychotic Seroquel mixed with different variations of Zoloft, Wellbutrin, Lexapro—all followed up by a daily ingestion of lithium. This prescribed cocktail of pharmaceuticals was topped off at night with a cherry on top. They gave me one of my favorite drugs—Ambien. This was so I could sleep my life away. After these combinations of prescribed meds, it is easy to assume those eight months were much of nothing. It was as if I was a character acting as an extra on a zombie apocalypse roll, barely coherent enough to breathe.

Knowing I was going to prison drove my feelings and emotions deeper down. You quickly learn that emotions are a weakness when entering those barbed wire fences with armed guards. Many of the men who are incarcerated have little or no reason to live anymore. The men who show any weakness become targets, quickly to be taken advantage of, often as quickly as they enter those walls. I had to hide my emotional turmoil. I buried it deep inside the moment the handcuffs were tightly clasped on my wrists, the exact moment I was escorted to my first holding cell after the judge sentenced me. Nothing would ever be the same. Any sign of love for others was buried upon entering those walls, or so I thought. I had no idea that I would begin loving myself more and more after being incarcerated.

LOVING MY STRUGGLE

From 2003–2014, roughly 3,800 days of my life, all that mattered to me was beating the prison system. For those ten-plus years, nearly every waking moment was aimed at beating the system and learning how to take my anger out on the system by proving them wrong. I was on a mission to prove all the correctional officers that talked shit and treated us like shit were wrong. I wanted to prove all the case management workers who only saw a DOC number and not a person—wrong. Every halfway-house employee who thought they were better than the men and women in their facilities—wrong. I even wanted to prove to all the inmates, who spend their lives in and out of the system, afraid to change, afraid to work hard, and afraid to love their lives and love themselves—wrong. Many inmates believe they can never survive as a normal person outside of the fences. I wanted to prove to them that it could be done. My mentality was different than all of theirs. Deep down, I knew I was going to do something special, though I didn't know what it was. During those years, I woke up every day with this looming bureaucratic system of a black hole hovering over me. Prison has a tendency to suck the lives out of inmates, rarely letting them go. I fought every day to beat the system. I fought every day to not be a statistic. I fought every day to be better than I was the day before. It was a challenge. I loved that challenge of proving everyone wrong. I was an underdog. There was joy in the process because I had direction. Yet, during that time, I never looked inside my heart. I was motivated by fear of failure, fear of being a statistic, fear of being a never-have or never-will-be. God had a different plan.

During those ten-plus years in the system, never did I ever think about loving myself. Life was a game, prison was a game, and all I cared about was winning. During that process, I never learned to love myself. Accomplishing goals and proving people wrong was my focus. I loved beating the odds and going from an inmate to a college basketball player to the best student on campus, all while a part of the Department of Corrections. Everything was a goal, an objective to check off. Nothing was about being in the present and living. Not once did I ever think about loving myself.

That all changed one summer day when I received one of my uncle's random calls. "Hey dickhead, are you home?" I replied to him, "Yes, douche bag," or some other nasty comment not made for this book. About an hour later, my weird, bizarre, funny uncle showed up to the house I shared with my brother. After hours of our typical mix of deep conversations and bizarre, weird ones, he looked at me and said, "You're killing yourself." Something inside of my uncle was telling him that I couldn't last much longer going at this pace without burning out. I'm sure his biggest fear of my burnout would be me going back to the bottle again. At the time, I blew it off as one of his lazy ways of living, yet something resonated with me over the next few days. He was right. I was killing myself. Prior to this conversation, I was working sixty to eighty hours per week, in grad school full-time, an assistant basketball coach at my old university, and starting my own speaking career. Before that conversation, I had spent the last seven-plus years straight sleeping less than four hours a night, seven days a week. My mind was on accomplishing everything and trying to be everything. During all this, not once did I ever talk about my mental health, not once did I ever discuss the harm I was putting my body through. He opened that conversation. My uncle is one of those AA voices of wisdom. He's good for a few of those conversations every year. I love the fact I can have deeper, more meaningful conversations with him than nearly anyone else. He's probably the closest person I have on this planet and want him to know through this book how much I love and care for him. So, here's your kudos, dickhead. :)

A few days after our conversation, I began thinking about what hours I could start cutting from work, school, or coaching. Where could I allot a few hours a day to just relaxing, watching a movie, or playing a video game for fun? I needed a change, and he was right. I needed to cut back on something. The deeper I dove into my life, the more I began realizing I needed to take care of me. My focus began on my mental health. My focus began on prioritizing my foundation. During this process, I began to love myself, love the life I was creating versus everything just being a job, a goal, or something to obtain. For years, people had always asked me if I knew how to smile. A smile would rarely be seen on my face outside of playing basketball and joking with teammates or family. I ultimately decided to lessen my constant twenty-hour-per-day workload down to about twelve hours per day to avoid burnout. I was learning to love myself.

CALL TO ACTION

Answer this one uncomfortable question:

- Do you love yourself?

If the answer is no to this simple yet difficult question, sit down and write out a list of all the positive things you bring to the world. Highlight the positive moments you bring to others, the moments you make others happy, smile, or laugh.

Once you find those moments and write them down, take a few moments and tell yourself over and over that you are a good person and you bring value to this world. Start to find positive aspects in your life so you can learn to love who you are and what you are all about.

CHAPTER 19

TAUGHT TO WEAR A SUIT OF ARMOR

Countless men on this planet are raised to hide their feelings, taught to be indestructible, and told to display as little weakness as possible. They never learn to convey or express their feelings, as it's seen as a weakness. On the surface, they are told to appear vigilant through the roughest of times, like generations of old. Expressing feelings means you are a pussy, weak, and soft. Vulnerability is a term not thrown around for many men, especially men in athletics, construction, military, police, or prison. Being open and transparent has been viewed as a sign of frailty until the last few years. Our society has shifted the conversation around mental health and vulnerability, and I believe it's a good thing. It's a characteristic of my job to be a continual voice that breaks down the reluctance of vulnerability in men.

It's okay to fail. We will all fail at something. We will all struggle at some point in our lives, I truly believe that. What's not healthy in the long term is harboring pain and trauma inside, choosing to live in isolation from the feelings held deep within. I speak from experience. I pushed away my wife because of my lack of vulnerability during the pandemic. I shut down instead of opening up like I had done in the first two-thirds of our marriage. At some point toward the last third of the pandemic, I reverted to isolation instead of discussing my struggles. I chose to avoid expressing my feelings, showing no signs of emotions, trying to protect her from my negative state of mind, and it grossly backfired. She now avoids me like a sick person with COVID and monkeypox at the height of contagion. Again, this book fits into that adage, "Do as I say, not as I do." I've made countless mistakes in my life, but because I'm willing to be vulnerable about these mistakes, it helps me heal, allowing me to move forward because I'm trying versus giving up, like a large portion of society does.

Kevin Love was the first professional athlete that I recall opening up about his mental health struggles. This was around 2018. Love openly discussed his experience with anxiety and panic attacks during the NBA playoffs. It was an eye-opening moment for millions who struggled silently with their own battles, thinking they were the only ones dealing with these issues. I wish some athletes would have taken this very same leadership role on mental health in 1999–2003 when I was contemplating death by suicide on most nights. There were no role models in the mental health arena. The mentality was "There is nothing wrong with me. Stop being weak. Be strong, and nobody cares about your weak-ass feelings." If you showed any feelings, the strong would take advantage of you. When professional athletes, actors, actresses, and entertainers open up about their vulnerabilities and show that it's okay to talk about things, it provides leadership, allowing the masses to feel safe. If your favorite athlete is willing to discuss their struggles with open vulnerability, you are more likely to have the propensity to do the same.

If the best athletes in the world, our gladiators of today, can be vulnerable, why can't the corporate world? It's been taboo to show vulnerability at the top of the corporate world. C-suite executives are the top men and women of the workforce who have climbed their way to the top by being ruthless, stubborn, and efficient, often putting their career goals ahead of all others. They've been conditioned to not exhibit their vulnerabilities. The top brass has a tendency not to hire those they see as weak or who complain about their personal lives on the company's time. Leaders in management rise to the top by generally being hardened individuals, making the hard decisions, showing little or no fear, and leading by an iron fist. Rather than showing vulnerability, business leaders have practiced what social psychiatrists call "impression management"—also known as "fake it till you make it." Toby Thomas, CEO of EnSite Solutions (No. 188 on the Inc. 5,000), explains the phenomenon with his favorite analogy: a man riding a lion. "People look at him and think, this guy's really got it together! He's brave!" says Thomas. "And the man riding the lion is thinking, how the hell did I get on a lion, and how do I keep from getting eaten?"[1] Employees see corporate leaders conquering the corporate world. The man riding the lion is scared to death. He doesn't know who he can be vulnerable in front of without being seen as a failure or weak. In turn, he keeps all this turmoil, doubt, and fear inside, not realizing the internal effects stress takes on the body. He's slowly killing himself, all because he is afraid to be vulnerable about the fear of riding on the back of the lion.

ANGER, EMBARRASSMENT, AND COUNSELING

My emotions have a tendency to get the best of me. In the past, I would try to hide my feelings as much as possible from the outside world, keeping them deep inside under lock and key—fitting the general mold and stereotype of a "strong athlete" or a "man's man" growing up. It feels like the only emotion a man's man can freely display without feeling weak is anger. This is where I excelled. I had boatloads of anger. At times, I had too much anger mixed with pride and cockiness flowing through my veins. It negatively impacted my life and those around me. My anger was a dangerous cocktail of emotions, at any given second ready to strike like a black mamba, verbally abusing my victims. Most often it was my family and friends who would receive the brunt of my anger. My own fears, insecurities, and terrified mind of suicidal ideations would be placed on others. My depression from self-loathing and self-hate from the inside was spewed out on others by using hate and anger. It was destructive. It's sad to say I'm not the only one; it's what many people do. They take their own insecurities out on others using anger. That's why bullies are bullies. Many are struggling with their own deeply rooted insecurities, and instead of addressing their traumas or pains, they take it out on their victims.

Embarrassment was another catalyst and motivation to keep my feelings inside. I never wanted to be portrayed as weak or somebody to be taken advantage of. Like many struggling individuals, I tended to keep my emotions close to the chest, allowing them to suffocate me unless I let them out. When I let my struggles out, my darkness seemed to suffocate others, so I kept it even closer to the chest. Those around me did not like being around so much pain, darkness, and negativity, so they avoided deeper conversations, which made my friendships with them superficial and unimportant to me. I've lost many relationships due to my negative thinking and their lack of ability to deal with my thoughts, one reason I have a very small, if not mostly nonexistent, circle of friends.

People are often fake, saying they want to help in times of need, but when you burden them with your pain and struggles, they don't know how to react, so they become avoidant and distant. Therefore, counselors and trained professionals are critical in the path to recovery. Counselors are trained to absorb and openly discuss your negative emotions, whereas many friends will not be prepared for that emotional turmoil.

Over time, I have worked hard to quell these negative thoughts and patterns with some great success, largely due to the five keys and the next chapter's topic of "gratitude." My ability to express more than anger, depression, and sadness has all changed—now my life is completely different. It started by standing on stage and being vulnerable about all my emotions. The desire, love, passion, and purposeful meaning I began receiving from audiences opened the door to vulnerability. Sharing my story has led me to be open about my struggles, when in prior years they were locked away.

In 2003, I was diagnosed with social anxiety, which would leave me nearly paralyzed in public situations. It's still a major struggle to be around people. In my first few years of college, I intentionally failed classes so I wouldn't have to speak in front of my classmates of fifteen to thirty students. Mind you, these were not large events like entire school assemblies or entire corporate conferences like I've been keynoting these past few years, but these were small, close settings. I've come a long way since dropping out of class to miss presentations, which leads me to this chapter and vulnerability. I pour my heart out to the audiences and crowds—describing, visually showing the worst times in my life, attempting to paint the most realistic picture of the emotions that were bubbling inside of me at the time in my life that coincides with each slide in my speech. When I began opening up about the accident and showing the pain I was feeling inside every day, I started to heal. My vulnerability allowed me to heal.

Prior to the academic year of 2015–2016, my mental health was never a concern. Frankly, I didn't even know what mental health truly meant. "Mental health" wasn't a popular phrase at the time. In 2015, when I spoke to the athletics programs at the University of Northern Colorado (UNCO), one of my old college teams, it was the first time I had openly discussed my depression and suicidal ideations on the speaking stage.

It was a unique opportunity to stand on the basketball court in the Butler-Hancock Athletic Center where the UNCO Bears play and point out to the crowd of 400 student-athletes the exact spot on the floor where I mentally quit on the coach and my team. Little did the athletes know I would open up about my drunk nights and my suicidal nights on campus as I pointed in the general direction of the dorm I lived in, followed by the general direction of the first-ever counseling center I went to. It was the first time in front of a group that I had ever mentioned my internal embarrassment and shame I had as a college basketball player going to the counseling department because I wanted to die. I told the crowd, "I had my hoodie over my head, headphones

loud, hat over the brim of my face, avoiding any eye contact. I was bob-
bing and weaving in and out of doorways in the counseling center, trying to be a ninja or burglar, doing all I could not to be seen." It was one
of the most isolating moments in my life. I was under the impression I
was literally crazy if I was going to be seeing a counselor. In those days,
the stigma was just that. I didn't want anyone to know that about me.
At the time, visiting the counseling center was one the most embarrassing situations I could have imagined, especially as student-athlete.
Years later, I realized I created all the embarrassment in my own head.
My mind is the worst enemy I have; it's been waging war and winning
battles for as long as I can remember.

It took incredible strength and vulnerability to admit my decade-plus of a pent-up, locked box of emotion on Butler-Hancock's
basketball court at the time. This open vulnerability was something I
hadn't yet practiced, but it had been weighing on my mind for years. I
didn't know how the athletes would take it. Deep down, I was worried
that the athletes would think I was "crazy" and they wouldn't take me
seriously after I told them of my mental health battles. The only thing
that guided me that day was my heart, faith, and a moment of extreme
vulnerability. Putting my fearful secret out to the people in the crowd I
cared about was all that mattered—now that's vulnerability.

The reactions I received from all the student-athletes after the
event were priceless. Being vulnerable with my own mental health
struggles seemed to have opened the doors of the athletes' own awareness of their mental health struggles. As soon as they told me they
were going through similar battles internally and had nobody to talk
to until now, it was life-changing for them but even more life-changing
for me. From that moment on, I made a conscious effort to share my
feelings about my past and current mental health struggles with every
audience I could. I showed them the vulnerable side of me, and not just
my resilient ambition to beat the odds to play basketball again or my
fake hardcore demeanor many assume of me—this event was a true
"a-ha" moment.

HELPING OTHERS FIND VULNERABILITY

A strange number pops up on my phone. I pick it up expecting a spam call.

"Hello, Mr. Fisher. My name is…I got your number from our mutual contact after briefly meeting you the other night."

"Ohhh yeah. I remember you. How are you? How can I help?"

"I was told by one of the parents that saw your talks—they mentioned you might be a good contact to speak to. Can I ask you some questions about what you do and how you are helping young lives? Can you tell me a little about what you do?"

During the next ten-plus minutes, I explained my job and what I do. It's not hard to get me to talk about my career. I might be quiet and reserved, but when I'm asked about what I do for a living, my mouth and mind go into a selfish hyperdrive, and it's hard for me to stop talking about myself. I'm a tad narcissistic, but I have a feeling many motivational and keynote speakers are. After I got through talking about my career, I asked him how I could be of service.

He replied, "Our mutual friend told me that you are a good resource to talk to when people are struggling." He mentioned he recently lost an amazing job, was frequently fighting with his wife, and overall hated his life. Eventually, he told me that earlier that morning he had a line of prescription pills out on the bathroom countertops and planned to take them all at once. He was going to overdose and complete his suicide. By the grace of God, he didn't follow through with his plan. He mentioned not knowing why he didn't go through with it, but some fleeting thoughts of his amazing children or wife, or some thought or image of being happy, prevented him from going through with taking all the pills, and here he was talking to me, alive!

Over the phone, I could hear a massive weight lifted off his shoulders. All that pain he had bottled up inside, hidden from the world in order to not feel judged, altered not only his entire day but changed his perspective for the duration of his life. We talked about suicide, we talked about depression, and how it's okay to talk about these things. He was under the impression, like many men, that he was the only man struggling. He couldn't believe that other men felt this way. He couldn't believe men expressed these types of feelings. He was a grown-ass man who never thought others felt the same way as he did. Little did he know that I had a conversation with another male who was struggling in the same small mountain town days earlier. Toward the end of our call, I said, "You are in luck, my friend. I know of a men's group in your town that talks about these issues in private." I gave him the information needed to connect with that group.

Fast forward a few months later, he called me to check-in.

"Ethan, I just wanted to give you an update. I've got a new job, and my family is amazing. Thank you for being there for me. I've been going to the men's group, and it's helped me tremendously." This gentleman made a phone call that changed his life. He was vulnerable, and it ended up altering his path. Now he is a success story for himself. I hope he reads this and is proud of the man he's become.

It's ingrained in our brains at a young age that men are tough, men are durable, and men surely can't have "girly" emotions. It's my job to break down that stigma. I'm here to smash that mental block and societal stigma and say, "Hey, I'm struggling. It's okay to struggle. Life is hard, but we can all get through it." Trust me, I'm a strong-ass dude, but I feel so much better when I can be open about the crap I feel inside. It helps. As men, we don't have to feel soft when we talk about emotions. I cry like a baby often, and it was embarrassing at first to admit, but now I freely do it on stage in front of thousands of strangers. It gives me strength and changes the lives of those who see my tears. Audiences know I am human and just like them. I'm stronger at discussing and showing emotions. Guess what? I'm no punk bitch either.

Being vulnerable is letting others see the pain and struggle you're going through. It's telling others of your fears, hopes, and your big dreams. Being vulnerable is extremely difficult. Letting people in to see the truth, no matter the outcome or hit to the ego, is the ultimate display of vulnerability. Letting others into your personal life, and not just your social media posts of all the great things you do, is true vulnerability.

CALL TO ACTION

Challenge: Admit you're wrong. Admit you're feeling pain.

Admitting that you were wrong or that you did something you shouldn't have done is difficult.

- Take some time and write down a list of some of the poor choices you've made that impacted your life or impacted your immediate family, friends, or coworkers.

- Think hard and deep dive into a specific decision that you have made or a situation that you have put yourself in in the past. A time that you know you were wrong but never admitted it. Take a piece of paper and write the scenario down, asking yourself these questions: What did I do wrong? What could I have done differently? Whose fault was it?

- Take accountability for your choices and actions, realizing you could have made other choices that would have impacted that moment differently.

If you can't be honest, true, and vulnerable with yourself, how will you be vulnerable with others?

- After you finish writing this down, reach out to the person you wronged. Tell them you are sorry for what you caused, taking accountability for your past choices. Tell them you made the wrong decisions and allowed your emotions to get the best of you.

- Ask for forgiveness and move toward a healthier relationship and life with that person.

I have done this process with my ex-wife, and it has allowed me to move on. I wrote her multiple lengthy letters stating my wrongs, taking accountability for my actions. I'm content that I tried and hope she forgave me for my actions. It didn't lead to reconciliation. As a matter of fact, I've never heard a word from her since. But I feel like I let it all out and don't have this "what if" feeling burning inside any longer. I'm at peace because I know I admitted my wrongs.

CHAPTER 20
GRATITUDE

"I'm grateful for having gratitude."

– JAY-Z

Without gratitude, nothing matters. Chances are, if you are not grateful for the little things you have in this world, you will continue to struggle in life. There is scientific research and data out there proving gratitude improves your overall disposition in life, including your foundation and mental health. When I was younger, I had very little appreciation for anything. I was never grateful for the amazing things in my life, and I had it pretty good as a kid. After the accident and my time in prison, my mind shifted. A new appreciation for being alive grew, and along with that change, my life began to improve. I had a unique opportunity to start a new life after prison, and I did just that. I started a new path, a new chapter, and a new direction. With this new change, I was ready to embrace life and take on the challenges of the world.

For over seventeen years, this appreciation and gratitude flowed throughout my life. Then it wore off. Frankly, it's heartbreaking writing this statement, but during the pandemic, I lost my daily gratitude practices. I began to take everything for granted, allowing depression and negativity to ruin my life. Guess what? My life began to fall apart without gratitude. In this chapter, I hope to convey just how important gratitude is, not only to my success but to your success as well.

Earlier in the book, I discussed the importance of writing out your goals and that the likelihood of achieving your goals substantially increases just by writing them down. The same holds true for gratitude. Writing down and expressing what you are grateful for alters the brain and increases your chances of being happy and content with your life. When times are rough, pick up a pen and write out what you are grateful for. Your mood will change.

Brown and Wong did a study with three hundred adult college students who were facing mental health issues before their first counseling session. They broke down the three hundred test subjects into three groups. The first group wrote gratitude letters and sent them out, the second group wrote gratitude letters but did not send the letters out, and the third group didn't do any gratitude writing. What they found was those who wrote letters reported significant improvements in their mental health after only twelve weeks. Simply writing down what the test subjects were grateful for improved their mental health. Brown and Wong also determined four key insights from their study that display the positive effects of writing gratitude out. The first was that the process of writing helps rid the body of toxic emotions by using less negative emotion words, which increased the participant's positive mental health. The second helpful insight that they found was that writing positively affects the brain, even if the participants didn't send the gratitude letters out. The third insight was that the benefits of gratitude writing do take time, and they do not happen overnight. Lastly, they found that gratitude has lasting effects on the brain. They performed fMRIs on the participants of the survey and found that there was greater activation in the prefrontal cortex in those who wrote gratitude letters versus those who didn't write gratitude letters.[1]

Simply practicing gratitude literally alters the brain. Spending a few minutes a day writing down what you're grateful for rewires your brain. It's something so simple yet has astounding effects on the brain and your happiness. According to "The Neuroscience of Gratitude and Effects on the Brain," gratitude reduces anger and depression in those struggling with mental health issues. Gratitude reduces stress hormones and manages the autonomic nervous system functions. Gratitude significantly reduces symptoms of depression and anxiety.[2] A little gratitude can go a long way toward improving your attitude, your moods, and altering your brain's network. Mental health is at the core of this book and a huge piece of your foundation. Practicing gratitude is a great tool to have in the battle against mental health challenges.

GRATEFUL FOR FREEDOM

Incarceration can be a very serious detriment to life. With the appropriate positive attitude of gratitude, the horrible situation of prison can be turned around into a unique appreciation. Prison was a very difficult and challenging time in my life. Every day in those cells, or time spent in the DOC military boot camp, or fighting forest fires as a firefighter, I woke up with a positive mindset because I was grateful for being alive. I repeatedly told myself *I should have died that night in the accident.* Knowing I was blessed to be alive and that my outcome could have been much different, I was happy to still be here. This mentality afforded me the appreciation for the fact that I was still breathing.

I went into prison scared and afraid of the environment I was going to spend the next chapter of my life in. It was up to me and only me to determine how I handled the situation. I had to alter my thinking. I had to change my attitude while incarcerated. I didn't want to be a grown man hating his life after the experience I had just been through. Something deep inside of me wanted to rise from the ashes and become a different person. The process started by waking up every day, counting my blessings, and being thankful for the fact that I was alive. Anyone walking this earth can have the same mentality—we are all blessed to be alive—but it takes positive self-talk, confidence, endurance, and strength to continuously attempt to be grateful day in and day out. That is where people tend to get lost. Being consistent is difficult, especially when faced with roadblocks. That's why writing down your gratitude is important. It allows you to see all the positives you have in your life, helping you navigate emotionally through the difficult times and roadblocks.

Upon my release from prison, I was grateful for nearly everything: the fresh air, the freedom to sleep in my own bed, the comfort of wearing a pair of Jordan shorts, and the ability to go to the gym when I wanted to, not just when the prison "yard" was scheduled to be open to the general population. After my release, I was going to college and was excited to earn a degree. In full transparency, upon release, I was excited to see women for the first time in years. I was so happy to be free that I bought Gatorades from the gas station every day, just because I could. My Gatorade and energy drink habit was nearly as costly as buying cigarettes. Buying a Gatorade represented much more than dollars and cents—it was a simple reminder of my freedom. Having the ability to buy something that I hadn't had access to in nearly three years was a blessing. I was so happy and so content with the smallest of things after prison. My life was awesome. I had gratitude for the smallest of conveniences and appreciation for life in general. Life was good. Heck, life was great, and it didn't even matter that I had an ankle monitor on. It didn't matter that I couldn't leave my house until six a.m. and I had to be back in my house by nine p.m. That didn't matter to me. I was grateful for the blessing to be free and out of prison. I lived this way until 2020–2022—then my expectations changed, and the gratitude of being free began to wear off. I began expecting the little things versus being grateful for the little things. This is when the downfall began.

LOST GRATITUDE

In 2019, I was married to the most amazing woman and partner I could have asked for. Being married to her was the best thing to ever happen to me. It was pure elation mixed with nervousness and some fear of being married all at the same time. Things completely shifted in my life for the better. A new element of contentedness began filling my heart. It was the second time in my life where suicide didn't cross my mind. Marriage was a blessing and a gift until I began having expectations versus gratitude. During the pandemic, I no longer saw the little things as a blessing. I started having expectations of what was "supposed" to happen. When those expectations didn't get met, I lost track of the gratitude I previously had since the accident. I began having large exceptions about my speaking career, only to be wiped out during the pandemic. Those expectations caused me to become stressed, depressed, and were ultimately the catalyst in the destruction of my marriage. I lost sight of the little things my wife and I did together, like conversations in the kitchen, dinners together, taking walks with the dogs, and my favorite—napping on the couch with my ex-wife, the dogs, and our cat. But toward the last third of the pandemic, we began nitpicking at the small things versus appreciating them, and it slowly eroded our foundation as a married couple. I want to blame the pandemic, but the truth of the matter is I lost sight of my gratitude, leading to the failings of my marriage. I had too many expectations and not enough appreciation and gratitude for the small things. At the beginning of dating and marriage, I appreciated all the small things. It's disheartening to say this on paper, but my foundation was cracked. Something was off. I was empty inside and felt alone.

When I'm deep in reflection, I cherish and consciously think about what I'm grateful for, yet the old programming of dark thoughts and suicide floated around in my mind like nanoplastics in the ocean, slowly killing the creatures that accidentally ingest it while attacking their food for their survival. Figuratively, the nanoplastics were choking me, clogging my neural pathways and arteries. My divorce was killing me inside, but I portrayed this strong man on stage that I wasn't. I was dying inside, and nobody would save me except for me. My level of self-love had evaporated. I caused my wife so much pain by ignoring her that she asked for a divorce and kicked me out of the house. It's hard to love yourself at all when the best thing in the world you have ever had decided you are not lovable anymore. The process of divorce has been brutal. They've been the most emotionally damaging months of my life. I wish I could take it all back, but I can't.

I've reflected during the months since the separation, and I've begun focusing more on my gratitude—in turn, my spirits have lifted. It's as if a black cloud and fog were swept and blown away. It's easy to look back on the pandemic, realizing I lost my gratitude for life and, in the process, became so depressed that I forced my wife away from me because I wasn't grateful for her and the constructs of marriage.

Moving forward, I will not let that happen again. I wake every morning and give thanks to God that I'm alive and breathing. I've started putting the pen to the pad again, journaling about my gratitude and the little things I'm happy to appreciate. Every day I meditate. As of late, I've been tapping to a happiness meditation. This is a form of meditation that has you tapping on specific points on your body, repeating positive affirmations. I've noticed a significant difference in my mentality since becoming grateful again. It's like night and day. My only regret is that I failed to do so during the pandemic. Due to my lack of recognition, I'm now a separated, soon to be a divorcee, and I wish I wasn't.

Just like everything in this life, I will learn from my mistakes. I will learn from this massive failure and move forward. Even though I've experienced my darkest days during this separation and divorce, the ability to write down what I'm grateful for in my journals is helping me move forward. As you can see, there has been a substantial crack in my foundation, yet I'm still grateful to be alive. I'm still grateful to have been married, and I'm so grateful for my career. Even in the darkest moments, I still find bits of sunshine and realize I have an overall good life. It's all about perspective, and it starts with gratitude.

CALL TO ACTION

Start a journal of gratitude.

Every day, write down three to five things you are grateful for.

The more consistent you are, the greater your development and appreciation of gratitude will be. When I'm struggling, I turn to my journal and write down the aspects of life I'm grateful for. I try to include the smallest aspects of my daily life, from playing with my dogs to having food in the fridge (even if I eat like a broke college student). I know deep down I'm blessed and lucky to be alive. I sometimes lose track, but when I take the time to write them out, my reality of gratitude settles in, and I'm much more positive throughout the day.

PART 5

SUCCESS

Success is the final destination of this book's journey. What is it? Success will look different to everyone. How do you determine your success? Is it the amount of money in your bank account? The number of friends you have on Facebook, Instagram, or LinkedIn? Do you determine success based on work projects and climbing the corporate ladder? How do you define success in your personal life and your relationships? Everyone's definition of success will be different than the person's sitting next to them. It's up to you to determine what success is.

These last three chapters are about how I determine my successes. Firstly, I believe failure is one of the greatest gifts, a launching pad, a spark from a lighter for somebody to achieve new levels of success. It might sound counterproductive, but failing can push you into success. Secondly, confidence in what you do is also critical to the path of success. Without confidence in who you are and what you do in life, success will not likely follow. When you have confidence, chances are you can and will find purpose. When you have a mindset of purpose, life will have more joy, value, and excitement. Lastly, I believe forgiveness completes the journey from failure to success. We have all wronged others and been wrong ourselves. If we can forgive and move on, success will be much easier to maintain and keep.

I determine my successes by the impact I have on audiences and the number of events, speeches, and workshops I produce each year.

My success is not defined by how little money is in my bank account but by the lives I change. I determine my success by the thousands of letters I receive. Another significant piece of success for me is not drinking, not giving up, and to continue fighting for this purpose in my life. My success will look different from what you determine your success is.

CHAPTER 21

FAILURE IS SUCCESS WITH THE RIGHT ATTITUDE

"God designed us to make mistakes. But our schools
punish you for making mistakes."
– ROBERT KO

Everyone will fail at something! It takes courage to keep fighting. It takes courage to respond with determination and never give up. Failure is only a failure if you do nothing about it. Failure can drive individuals to great feats. Failure can motivate and inspire individuals to do amazing things. Failure can push an individual to levels of accomplishments they never dreamed of. On the flip side, failure can crush the mind, weaken the spirit, and destroy any hope. Your success will be determined by how many obstacles and roadblocks you overcome to achieve your goals and dreams.

Nobody walking this once-green earth, with its carbon dioxide-polluted skies, is perfect. It doesn't matter how many social media followers are on their platforms or how many zeros they have in their bank account, nor does it matter how large their trust funds and investment portfolios are. No one is perfect, even if many say they are. Everyone, I mean everyone, has flaws, everyone has mishaps, and anybody who has tried at something has failed at something else. If you are trying at anything, failure is inevitable.

It's okay to be depressed, it's okay to suffer from anxiety (like I mentioned in earlier chapters), and it's okay to fail. Failure is a part of life. The problem occurs when you hide the issues or avoid them by not fixing them with the appropriate treatments or solutions. Failure is an experience. It's how you move forward and take the next steps that matters. I see two choices in failure. Do you take that other L-word (loss or loser) and sulk around, defeated, and beat yourself up, quitting in the process? Or do you take that loss/failure, knuckle up, and fight to be better for the next go-around? Only you can make that choice. Choice=Life.

Accepting that you failed at something you love is a difficult thing to swallow. It can cause psychological pain, even physical pain. With some positive self-talk, you can make that moment of failure seem like an opportunity to grow. Failure will make you stronger. Failure will harden your mind. It will build strength by creating a layer of resiliency, a protective shield of strength to use when unexpected issues present themselves. If you choose to avoid failure, like we are taught in schools, and are too afraid or embarrassed to try anything, you will continue to struggle with mediocrity. Mediocrity is boring and sucks. There is too much this world has to offer to be mediocre. We all have the choice to do something great.

Failure because you didn't try is *not acceptable*—failing because you tried is. This is where the concept of "failing forward" should come into play. Failing forward is when somebody tries at something, fails miserably at it, yet walks away from the disappointment a better person because they tried. They will learn from that letdown. They will only choose to be bigger, better, and stronger at their next attempt. Failing forward is a great way to approach life. It's challenging to try new things that might make you uneasy or unsure of yourself, but you grow by failing and moving forward. I believe without failure there is no growth.

FAILURE SEEMS TO BE IN MY DNA

Hands down, I was a complete disappointment before the accident in 2003. "F" was not just my mid-term or final semester letter grades on my transcripts at nearly every college I went to before the age of twenty-four. My failures were never about failing forward. My failures were always for not trying and giving up. My entire career and purpose as a speaker forces me to look back at my past actions and use them as teaching lessons to educate those on what is not acceptable anymore. I've learned from most of my horrible mistakes and placed my lack of preparation for my basketball career into what matters to me the most—this amazing speaking career. I've sacrificed so much for this career. Countless hours of work, all my energy, pooling all my resources together to keep this momentum going and my relationships with schools and contacts growing. It's one of my professional goals to not look back and realize I didn't give it my all in this speaking profession. I will not quit or screw this career up like I screwed up all other aspects of my life. I won't allow past failures to muddy up the waters of this purposeful career.

Yet, with that statement mentioned above, failure must be a living, breathing organism swimming in my circulatory system. Failure appears to catch a ride on the back of my platelets, riding unhindered on the blood flow as it moves through my circulatory system. Failure seems to move with each beat of my heart, passing through my aortic valve and traveling thousands of miles through the insides of my arteries and veins. Failure appears to be second nature to me. My entire life seems to be filled with countless screwups. My life as a middle school student—failure. My life as a high school student—failure. My early life as a college student and college athlete—massive failures. My marriage was a failure. I'll never forget the moment my wife came downstairs and said, "I want a divorce." The next thirty to forty years of my life vanished in a matter of seconds. Literally, the greatest thing in my life and the best thing to ever happen to me no longer wanted to be married to me. That is Failure with a capital F—Failure personified.

Yet, after all these disappointments and valleys, I keep pushing. I keep failing forward to strive to be better the next day. I've learned to embrace my failures by helping others learn from my mistakes. I will continue in this new chapter of life to fail forward. Learning from the screwups I had in my marriage will make me better for the next time we are together or the next relationship I'm ever in. I'm determined to be the best husband or partner in any of my next relationships. Failing will make me a better partner and person, and I'm dedicated to failing forward for growth to become the best version of myself I can be—you can do the same.

FAILURE IN THE REAL WORLD, NOT JUST SOME BOOK TITLE TO SOUND SELLABLE

Think about this: the average person will have twelve different jobs in their lifetime. It's more than likely you will fail at a career, you will fail at a relationship. Heck, today half of all marriages will end in divorce. You will fail as a parent at protecting your child. You will do everything you can to help your precious seed stay away from the wrong crowd and hope they never drink or do drugs. Yet, the chances are high (no pun intended) that they will drink or use at some point in their lives. According to the CDC's Youth Risk Behavior Survey in 2019, twenty-nine percent of high school kids drank in the last thirty days, fourteen percent binge drank, five percent drove after drinking, and a staggering seventeen percent rode with a drunk driver.[1] That is an outrageous number of kids riding with drunk drivers. Hence why I believe my job as a keynote speaker is so important. I can prevent many of those drunk-driving moments with my story and programs.

Aside from the alcohol, drugs, and vaping, your daughter will eventually date a boy you can't stand. Your son will fall head-over-heels for a girl that you know will break his heart. You will try to warn him, but he'll pay no attention to you, thinking you've never had that same experience. He's in young love. At some point, your kids will scream and yell at you for no reason, even possibly say they hate you. This can be seen as a failure, but when you look back on your kids' lives, hopefully you will realize you kept them alive until they were eighteen years of age. That is far from a failure. You raised a helpless, whining, fragile, diaper-wearing infant into an adult, and no matter how much you don't think they are an adult, they are. You should be proud of what you've accomplished. Were there bumps and bruises along the way? Did you make mistakes? Yes, of course. But it's not a failure. If you gave up and didn't even try, I'm sorry to be blunt, but that is a failure. You've got to at least try.

It's not just your personal life that will see failure—business is about failure. The world is littered with businesses that have failed, and many of those people who started a business quit trying after one failure. According to the Bureau of Labor Statistics, only eighty-two percent of small businesses made it past their first year, another fifty percent will fail by year five, and another sixty-five percent by year ten.[2] Seems kind of like doom and gloom, but small business makes up 99.9 percent of the businesses out there and forty-four percent of the U.S. economic activity. There are 32.5 million small businesses in total. But guess what? All 32.5 million businesses faced points where thoughts of quitting occurred, yet they didn't. They kept pushing when times got rough. They faced countless disasters along the way, yet they didn't quit. Businesses fail, employees fail companies all the time, products fail, your friends and family will fail you. It's more than likely you will fail when starting a business or a new career. It's a high probability—does that mean you shouldn't try? No! It means be prepared for the struggle ahead and know hard times are likely to come.

IT'S HARD TO EMBRACE PAST FAILURES

I love who I am as a person. I wouldn't trade me for all the world. That includes all my failures, all my royal screwups, and all the regrets I have—trust me, I have many. People have told me I've experienced more failures than most, and I say, "I'm like a cockroach. It will take a nuclear bomb to kill me." I will not go away very easily. As I mentioned earlier, I believe in the "bend but I won't break" philosophy. Meaning I've come very close to quitting at basketball, life, marriage, and speaking, but I never actually quit. I've been bent like a contortionist, but I have yet to quit. I've experienced too many failures to stop trying. I know first-hand that failure breeds strength, and I will be even stronger when I come out of my latest failure.

Take a few moments and breathe. Take a moment and dive deep into some self-reflection. Ask yourself, at this moment, if you regret what you have done in life. Have you missed out on chances or opportunities that could have altered the outcome of your life? I know I have. There are many choices I've made that led to my biggest failures. If I could, I would redo them all over. Here are my biggest three failures for you to observe and learn from.

THE FIRST:

The earliest and biggest foundational regret I have was not receiving professional counseling in middle school. If I knew back then what I know now, I would have gotten the help I needed before I headed down a path of self-medication. Hopefully, this would have prevented me from drinking to mask my anxiety and depression, ultimately never drinking and getting behind the wheel of the Suburban the night of the accident and taking Bill's life, my biggest and most tragic regret. My life would be completely different if I didn't use weed or alcohol to self-medicate. I tell people all the time, if you need counseling, don't be afraid to get it. It works and can help alter your entire life. Don't wait any longer. Find the help you need now.

THE SECOND:

The most recent and biggest failure I wish I had the power to alter would be the erosion of my marriage. If I had the power to go back and change the past, I would pay more attention to my wife. I'd thoughtfully and intentionally dedicate several sweet, gentle touches, hugs, and kisses for her every day. I would have appreciated her instead of taking her for granted like I did the last few months of the pandemic. I needed to stop drowning in my sorrows when things weren't going well during the pandemic and love her, not focus on the world falling apart. I focused on the negativity, avoiding my own foundation, and I lost the greatest gift. I had all I needed in this world, but I took it for granted—a massive malfunction on my part.

THE THIRD:

The odds of me playing professional basketball were slim to none, but I regret not dedicating my life to chasing the dream with purpose and dedication. I chased the dream but failed to make the right choices around my mental health, alcohol, and drugs along the way. I'd go back and never drink or use drugs. I'd spend countless hours in the gym lifting, practicing, and training instead of partying with people I don't even know anymore. If I made it, my life would have felt complete. It's all I ever wanted. Plus, it would have been an amazing story, against all odds for a slow, skinny, outmatched point guard to make it. If I didn't make it, I could admit I tried my best and went for it. The reality of being a slow, five-foot-eleven white boy would justify my improbable and feeble attempt at pro hoops. In any case, I could look back and accept that I tried my best and dedicated my life to the dream I had instead of squandering every opportunity I had because I started neglecting my foundation in middle school.

I will never accept the loss of Bill's life, the pain I caused his family, the neglect of my wife, and the lack of commitment to my basketball life. Those are my biggest failures and regrets. There have been times that I've wallowed in misery, close to allowing them to destroy me, but for some reason they haven't. These failures are helping me build a bigger, stronger me. A fresh new layer of resiliency embraces me after every one of those failures. They hurt to my central core, yet I've learned from these massive failures and love who I am. Do I have bad, dark days and weeks, hating my life at times? Yes! Overall, I love who I am and wouldn't trade me for anyone else. Do I wish I never drank and never got in that vehicle and took Bill's life? More than anything. Do I want more money in the bank? Hell yeah. Do I want my wife back? Hell yeah. Do I wish I could still play ball? Hell yeah. But I understand that those were in the past, and all I can do is love and appreciate who I am now, even when it's tough. It helps when I have reminders of why I keep pushing forward. A student activities staffer said to me today, "The youth and the world need Ethan Fisher." I believe that as well, and I won't allow failure to block my path to success.

CALL TO ACTION

This will be the longest, most time-consuming call to action in the book—if you do it thoroughly for each of the five keys.

- Make a list of some of the aspects you have failed at in life, whether it be at school, a job, a friendship, a business, or marriage.

- After writing down that list, begin writing and applying the five keys from Part 3 like my example below. It's a very helpful process and will help you gain some clarity into why or how your selected failure took place.

Here is my example:

- I failed at my marriage. For all you men who don't take your relationships seriously or take your partner for granted, please read these thoughts and learn from my failure. I'm being vulnerable about my relationship because I don't want that to happen to you! This section is about failure, but it's also about vulnerability and telling yourself the truth. I just happen to put my truths on this page for the world to read.

- Accountability: Was it my wife's fault? *No.* Was she perfect? No. It would be easy to blame her for quitting on me. During the pandemic, I was financially, mentally, and spiritually struggling. I was at my lowest, and she bailed on me, and that hurts to the core, but she had her reasons.

I needed to leave the house more and make a little extra side cash. It would have helped me not feel so trapped in what I called my basement prison. Not a good feeling when your home office is referred to as a prison cell. The groundhog's day of the same routine influenced my depression, which led to me shutting down. To make the matter even worse, little did I know that the Prozac I was on would only make it worse. I lost track of all time, failing to realize how long my isolation and ignoring of her was. I didn't realize I ignored her for a couple of weeks. I thought it was only a few days here and there. I didn't think about how it impacted her. I was so caught up in my quicksand of problems that I pushed her out. Prozac made my libido disappear. I had zero drive for contact or sex. We rarely touched during the last few months together. What could I have done? I could have made a game out of touching her, charted how many times I touched her, hugged her, and loved on her, versus disappearing and not touching her at all. I'd give anything just to hug and kiss her right now, yet I know it's over, and I accept and hold myself accountable for my failed marriage.

- Goals: Did I make any relationship goals? Very few over the duration of our lives together. It wasn't until 2022, nearly three years into our marriage, that I made "relationship goals"—but it was already too late. Every year, just like millions of people, I write down my yearly goals on New Year's. I've been doing this since I got out of prison. All my goals have been business goals, speaking goals, and things I wanted to achieve while I was being told what I couldn't do for nearly eleven years in the DOC system. These were all my selfish goals. Goals I made with the mentality of "when I get free from DOC"—"what I will do" goals. There were only a few "relationship goals" that I ever wrote down, and even those goals were selfish travel goals. I never put forth the effort to make "our" goals a priority. I just assumed we would travel, buy new houses, new cars, and enjoy our lives together. I never took the time to plan goals with her. What a colossal fuckup. These were things I failed at, and, looking back, I realize I could have made changes earlier in our relationship by being more intentional about wanting to grow together. I'm sorry I failed you.

- Choices: Every moment of every day, we have hundreds, if not thousands, of choices to make. One of the easiest choices I could have made during the pandemic was to get out of the house and get an office space instead of working from home. I was very unproductive the last few months due to the boring routine I ultimately created for myself. That boring routine caused me to resent being stuck in our marital home. I felt trapped after two-and-a-half years of the pandemic, and I needed an out. A simple office outside of the home would have made a significant difference in our marriage.

Relationships are tough, especially when your partner wants what you've always struggled with—showing affection. Affection was looked down upon in my household. My parents never touched, kissed, or held hands around us. Obviously, this would influence how I grew up. I was under the impression that affection was for pussies. My old programming negatively impacted my favorite person in this world. Instead of changing for her, I chose to stick to that old programming. I could have made a single choice to hold her hand in public. If I would have just done it the first day we dated, chances are something like this would have been a non-factor in the big scheme of life. It's a failure on my part. Believe you me, if we'd had a second chance, I wouldn't have let her hand go—ever.

- Perseverance: Here's where I really screwed up. Over the years, I would go through phases of hugging and touching my wife every day for a week or more. Why? I knew she needed affection—she told me. So, I would try. That's not how I operated. I failed to realize she needed consistent emotional and physical love. I didn't need loving touches. I'd provide affection for four, five, six days, and then I would stop trying. I should have kept trying. I should have kept showing her affection versus quitting. I'm wifeless, lonely, and missing her because I gave up on the simplest of things instead of using that perseverance inside to please my wife.

- Faith: My spiritual connection with the man named Bill, who, in 2018, stayed to watch my event at a religious school and changed everything (detailed in the last chapter). The belief and faith in my job as a keynote speaker and storytelling speaker skyrocketed, yet pieces of me didn't have the same level of faith about the constructs of marriage. For years, I saw many people I grew up with go through divorce and thought it was so sad. Deep down, I planted seeds of doubt about marriage and began believing that scary number of fifty-three percent of marriages ending in divorce, so why wouldn't mine? This massive fear of failure in marriage was always at the back of my mind, but I was happily pushing that doubt and fear as far back as possible because I loved my wife to death. The pandemic struggles began to mess with my mind, depression altered my confidence in our marriage, and somewhere along the line, my mentality began to manifest, not just in my work life but in my partnership as well. At some point in the time between January 2021 and May 2021, I lost faith in myself, which sent me into a dark depression.

A few months later, my depression snowballed even more. As I began planting seeds of doubt and losing faith in my marriage, it slowly began to erode. My negative thoughts and fears of failure from my speaking life destroyed the best thing in my life, my best friend. Was she perfect? No. But she was perfect for me. I always told myself that she was, yet I didn't show her enough appreciation, and now I find myself hit with the worst sadness I've ever had. I'm dead inside.

Writing out these five keys to my failed marriage is cathartic for me. This is like my journal or therapist, allowing me to process this grief I've experienced these past few years. Being able to apply my five keys as examples of what I could have done differently helps me, but they are intended to serve as an example for the list you create. Accepting accountability for my faults versus blaming her is a great start. Deep down, I want to blame her—that's easy. She quit on us. She quit because I broke her trust, shattered her love. Something switched in her, and she began protecting herself. I was supposed to protect her, yet she felt the need to quit. She was unhappy watching me waste away in that basement prison, and she wanted out. I must live with this massive *failure*.

Will I quit at life? No. Will I learn from it? Yes. Will I continue to push toward my goals? Yes. I won't give up on life. I have a purpose to live and a purpose to breathe—helping and serving others is the only thing keeping me going at this low moment in my life. Life is all about embracing your *failures*, which, sadly, I've become a master at. I feel like failing is a part of my DNA, yet I always bounce back because I embrace it and learn from it. It might take some time before I bounce back, but I will bounce back with a vengeance. My next relationship will be one I work at—I will make the changes I need to make it work. I've learned from my mistakes. Will I make mistakes in the next one? Of course. But I won't repeat the failures I had in my first marriage.

CHAPTER 22

CONFIDENCE—SKILLS TO PAY THE BILLS

Beauty, intelligence, talent, and skills are fantastic characteristics to possess, often giving a leg up on the competition. The world is filled with talented individuals. In my years as a traveling keynote speaker, I've met hundreds of amazing people with incredibly inspiring stories. I'm also aware that there are even more individuals walking the streets who have way more important and incredible stories than most of the "motivational" speakers out on the speaking circuit, myself included. We walk by individuals every day who have inspirational, motivating, and moving stories, and they are comfortable staying within the status quo. There are tons of musicians, comedians, painters, and actors who quietly sit in their households with major talent yet never let the world see or hear their beautiful souls. They allow only a select few the ability to hear or see their amazingness, as they decide to hide their skills from the world.

An individual can have all the talent in the world, but if they lack ambition, drive, and confidence to do anything about it, it's all for naught. If an individual lacks confidence, then every ounce of their talent and skills doesn't matter. It takes discipline, it takes desire, it takes a drive inside to chase your talents and turn them into a purposeful career. The reality is, the masses are too afraid of the work and risk associated with taking a chance on themselves. Many are afraid and don't want to be seen as failures. These hidden lives will never be discovered, never be sought after, and never showcase their talents to the world for fear of failure or because they lack the needed confidence to showcase their talents.

PRACTICE, PRACTICE, PRACTICE

How do you find confidence in anything? Practice, practice, practice. In the sports world, you do extra repetitions to build up your ability, your skill, which leads to improvement of your self-confidence. The path to building confidence begins after thousands of repetitions. In 2012, I began dipping my tippy toe into this speaking career, never fully understanding that it would become my entire purpose in life. At the start of this career, I lacked every ounce of confidence, ability, talent, skill, and process needed to become successful in the speaking industry. The single element that kept me relevant just long enough to be effective was my ability to speak from the heart. Outside of speaking from the heart, I lacked all confidence and had zero professional skills when it came to this career path I chose to take. To overcome my fear and lack of skill, I practiced my speech repeatedly, thousands of times, slowly and eventually building confidence in my speaking skills over time. Now I know I have the confidence to say I'm a great speaker, even won an award for it, yet I'm humble enough to admit I still have so much more to learn. Still to this day, I continue to practice my speeches for days, if not weeks, before each event to build my confidence in my material.

One of the early adopters of my story was author and speaker Tommy Spaulding. Tommy is a three-time *New York Times* Best Seller. Tommy is one of the most sought-out speakers in the world on the corporate speaking circuit. Every summer since 2014, Tommy has been gracious enough to invite me as a speaker to his National Leadership Academy (NLA). NLA is an academy for high school students that

Tommy created to develop leadership skills in youth from all over the county. Tommy has built more of a following than just a leadership academy. It's a transformational journey for one hundred fifty to two hundred students every summer who want to change their lives, and not just in leadership or serving like a good Samaritan in the community. The intended outcomes of this leadership academy are far different than most leadership retreats. NLA alters the lives of everyone who participates. It's much different than what they expect when they show up on day one. The most important trait of the long weekend is *love*, and secondly, vulnerability!!! Not your typical leadership academy vibes, I would say. Students learn to lead with their hearts by loving and being vulnerable with themselves while learning how to love and serve others. It's a unique and special opportunity that very few students will ever get the opportunity to experience. It's one of my favorite events every summer. Over the years, I've personally witnessed countless tears flow from the tear ducts of the young, impressionable minds. It's like watching gigantic barriers and protections come crashing down like the Berlin Wall. Individuals begin letting their true vulnerabilities come to the surface, allowing them to begin breaking down the armor that once protected them their entire lives. Nearly every student and staff who volunteers for NLA allows their walls to fall at some point throughout the long weekend. It is truly remarkable watching these youth overcome a handful of their fears while addressing their trauma from the past. Students enter NLA as hesitant, shy cocoons and blossom into magnificent butterflies by the last day, Sunday. During those quick four days, you can see the confidence oozing off many of the students as they prepare to take what they learned home with them and spread their confidence in love and vulnerability to their schools. They are changed, and changed to be better.

Tommy invited me to speak at NLA for the first time in the summer of 2014. Tommy had never seen me speak at that point; he had only heard my story through our conversations. Tommy knew and understood my heart, something he is exceptional at. He has built an incredible career on understanding the heart of others. He spent time with me discussing my plans to be a speaker but had not yet seen the product, taking a gigantic leap of faith in me. I'll forever be grateful for that. I was beyond nervous that first time speaking there. Here is one of the most booked speakers in the world, and I was keynoting on his behalf for his youth leadership academy. As you can imagine, I was nearly pissing down my leg. At the time, Tommy knew the power of my story but had zero idea of how poor a speaker I was at that point in time. My keynote was raw and powerful, yet needed so much work. It was probably dreadful for him to see me that first time, but I'm so thankful he continued to believe in me even after seeing my speech. Deep down, I believe he knew I would only get better. Fast forward five years later to the summer of 2019. Things had changed drastically for me as a speaker. I had done hundreds of events and practiced thousands of times since 2014. I was different. I possessed confidence which I had lacked in years prior.

For the previous four years I spoke at NLA, Tommy would follow up my speech with the story of how we met and talk about the momentum of forgiveness. In the summer of 2019, he spoke about more than the typical story from years past. As he stood with the microphone in his hand, in front of the crowd of people who adore him, he began speaking, gripping the audience with his loving embrace and tone. After his normal stories, he turned, looking over at me and then back to the crowd. In only Tommy fashion, with a burst of excitement and energy, he said, "When I first met Ethan and saw him speak, he was the *worst* speaker I had ever seen." Everyone in the audience laughed, and he laughed as well. This hit me deep to the core and was unexpected, but then the room quieted in dramatic fashion as the audience hung onto his every word. Tommy poured his heart out to the audience with a loud and proud, "Now look at him (long professional keynote speaker pause). He's the best speaker here!!!" Talk about an unexpected injection of super strength. My confidence level skyrocketed through the roof at that moment. Here is one of the most successful keynote speakers in the world, with thousands of high-paying keynotes for some of the largest Fortune 50, 100, and 500 companies in the world, and he's saying great things about my speaking abilities. Tommy's comments sent a substantial increase in dopamine and endorphins through my brain, instantly leveling up my confidence as a speaker. From that point on, I've truly believed I'm one of the top youth speakers in the country. The next goal on the list is to be one of the top speakers in corporate America as I come to your business and company to challenge, inspire, and motivate your employees from my teaching moments in this book. This magical transformation didn't happen overnight. I wasn't born with the gift of gab or natural ability to be on stage. Speaking to others has always been a problem.

In first grade, I was too afraid to raise my hand to stop my bus driver when he missed my bus stop. In doing so, the bus driver proceeded to drive another forty-five minutes up the Poudre Canyon and another forty-five minutes back down the canyon in order to take me home that day, all because I was too afraid to say anything to him. That should have been a sign moving forward that I was bound to have some social issues. It wasn't until I was twenty-three years of age that I would find out just why I was the way I was. After going to a psychiatrist in 2003, I was diagnosed with social anxiety disorder, meaning I have a difficult time being around people, especially groups with four or five individuals or more. Crowds leave me nearly paralyzed at times. After my diagnosis, I had a legit idea of why I was afraid of being in groups of people and crowds. I wish I would have learned this at a much younger age because it could have helped me have context around my social anxieties sooner. I still struggle with going into public, going to sporting events, going to the mall, and even going to airports. I avoid large crowds and tend to isolate from the world, a little too much at times. It's something I'm constantly working at and forcing myself to experience.

It's taken a massive desire to overcome my fear of groups and being in public to become a keynote speaker. It's been a challenging process.

Over the years, I've practiced thousands of speeches at my home office with nobody around to gain confidence in my ability to be on a stage. It's taken hundreds of volunteer speeches and small school stages to overcome my stage fright. It all circles back to practice, practice, and more practice. Nothing happens overnight; there are no overnight sensations. It took years of practice, years of failures to slowly build my confidence in speaking. Slowly, brick by brick, speech by speech, the quality of my programs continues to grow each year. The more I focused and worked at my purposeful profession, the more my skills and craft improved. Each time I speak, I work on improving and building my confidence along the way. The more times I'm in front of an audience, the more my overall confidence grows and evolves. It takes countless hours and repetitions to build confidence, and now I have the utmost confidence in my ability to move crowds.

AS J-ROSE WOULD SAY, "IRRATIONAL CONFIDENCE"

In life, no matter the type of career, educational background, profession, or level of sport played, confidence is critical for *anyone* to excel and succeed. A person with low self-esteem and low confidence will struggle with the smallest issues. Their "stinking thinking" thought process takes over. Those minor issues and lack of confidence will eventually gain traction, derailing the individual off their path to success.

Lacking confidence is something I've understood throughout my years. It started with the small negative thoughts in middle school. My negative, ruminating thoughts about being shy and scared to make friends impacted my confidence. I was afraid to be myself and fearful of not being a cool kid. This negative thinking grew and festered until I was afraid to talk to girls; I was even afraid to talk to new friends. If I'd obtained any steady amount of confidence in middle school/high school, I'd be living in a completely different parallel universe. My life would look one thousand times different than it does today. If it wasn't for sports, I would have been one of the least confident kids in any of my schools. Sports was the only thing I had any confidence in. Everywhere else, I was a scared little mouse.

On my recruiting trip to my one and only college basketball scholarship offer out of high school, I was destroying the players who were at the workouts. My confidence was sky-high. I signed my scholarship and was committed. Then preseason started. It was the first time I ever felt that I wasn't good enough to compete, and I lost my way in the first month of practice. I couldn't buy a bucket, I felt slow and outmatched, and my confidence was destroyed. I lost my starting spot before the season even started. My basketball confidence hadn't been that low since I was a kid. I remember calling my dad on the dorm pay phone and saying, "I can't play at this level." He did what a good father would do and told me to keep fighting. I remember him using one of his favorite quotes that day, "The cream always rises to the top." He knew my skills would rise to the level of play I needed to be at. Luckily, something clicked after losing my starting spot, and deep down, a fuel was ignited. I wasn't going to give up. I kept telling myself, *There is no way I'm not starting.* I changed my thinking from a self-defeating "poor me" attitude to the competitor I have deep inside of me. My self-talk started to be positive and driven with intention. I made a goal to get my starting spot back. I kept telling myself, *Keep working hard. You've trained your entire life to be here. You are good enough—just keep pushing forward.* Eventually my self-talk boosted my confidence, and I was able to regain my starting spot by the first regular game of the year. It all started with changing my negative thought-loop patterns into positive thought-loop patterns. Eventually, I regained the confidence I needed to be the player I sought to be. After changing my thinking, I was rewarded not only with the starting spot but a moment I'll never forget.

Literally, my first play of my college basketball career was an alley-oop pass from half-court off the jump ball. My very first play of my college career was an alley-oop. How cool is that? That play goes down as one of my fondest memories of any college game. After throwing the oop to Jamaal, I looked up at my dad as if saying "thank you" and proceeded to think college hoops was going to be easy from that point moving forward. I was humbled quickly, as we would eventually lose by 20-ish points in our own gym against a team that had a few of my good friends and high school teammates on it.

For obvious reasons, my bias leans heavily on sports as one of the biggest equalizers in a person's life, especially for kids. It's not just sports but any positive social group such as band, 4-H, or theater—all are incredibly important in a youth's development. Children who grow up in fractured homes, who are abused, mistreated, or told they are stupid will more than likely have a difficult start to their lives. But, through all that pain and struggle, they can excel in sports, they can excel in school, or excel in group activities, which in turn will boost their self-confidence and ability to remain resilient in future endeavors. If it wasn't for sports boosting my confidence along the way, I would have never made it through college, and I sure as hell wouldn't have made it through prison. I would have had a completely different experience in prison if I lacked confidence in who I was as a person and athlete.

WHY MY PURPOSE OF SPEAKING CONFIDENCE IS SO HIGH

"I've been suffering from depression since birth, and suicide has been an issue to me often. Any little thing can make me break down. I've tried to slit my wrist twice. I didn't want to go through with it because of my amazing friends and family. I've tried to starve myself and I have trouble talking to a therapist. I'm also embarrassed by it. What I'm trying to get at is, if you could please give me ways to keep my mind from these thoughts. Thanks, have a nice day." –Student

This is just one example of the thousands of emails I've received over the years. These testimonials are a huge reason for *why* I'm a speaker. These letters motivate me to continue to push through the growing pains and struggles of the business side of this speaker life. These testimonials are the reason I get up every day; they are the reason I believe I'm still alive. My purpose is to help and serve others who are struggling. I pour my heart out to every school or corporate audience I stand in front of with the hopes of altering one person's entire life. I change lives! I have the confidence to blurt that out to the entire world. A few years ago, I wouldn't have had the confidence to say that to the public—now I do.

There is something powerful in my speech. Is it the authenticity or vulnerability I display? Whatever it might be, it seems to reverberate in the minds of the ones who needed my message at that time. Often, I have a line of students waiting over an hour to tell me "thank you," shake my hand, or just say "hi." Many students come to me with a new sense of empowerment, yet they still feel embarrassed and reluctant to tell me their stories. Many times, their stories bring me to tears when I get back to the hotel. No youth should have to live a life of struggle and pain like many of the stories I hear. My heart hurts for them. All I want to do is help the struggling individual. Speaking often opens up the Pandora's box of pain they've been suppressing for years, if not their entire lifetimes. The individuals who tell me their stories are finding some inner strength to talk to a stranger, confessing the darkness and pain they've experienced. It's difficult to hear.

Teachers, counselors, social workers, and any person who works with at-risk youth have my respect and appreciation. I can't imagine how these individuals maintain their strength day-in and day-out. When I'm done at a school, I'm exhausted. I can't imagine that feeling every day, and for little pay.

Why am I writing about these emails in this section of the book? These emails give me the utmost confidence in why I do my job. If it wasn't for these emails and the impact I make, I would have quit this speaking career a long time ago. The business side of speaking sucks. I dislike it very much—all I want to do is speak. But the reality is ninety percent of the work I do is the process of getting events—and it's draining. These emails boost my morale, helping me keep my confidence up when the business side of this career tries to bring me down. My confidence is built by practicing my keynotes and by the testimonials I receive from audiences. I know this is what I'm supposed to do in this life, and I will continue to work toward my goal of inspiring millions of lives.

CHAPTER 23
LIVE WITH PURPOSE

Purpose tends to be understood as a higher calling, a belief that you are alive for a reason. For many millions of people, purpose is associated with God or some organized religion. For others, it's a spiritual power that gives a sense of well-being to those destined for a bigger plan. I'm under the impression, and truly want to believe, that I fall under the third statement. I faithfully believe, with the deepest of trust, that I'm alive for a reason! There is something greater than myself at the hands of my life. There must be a reason why I didn't die on those countless nights I intentionally tried to drink or drug myself to death. Unequivocally, I should have died the night of the accident, not Bill. He didn't deserve to die. Not an innocent fifty-seven-year-old husband, father, grandfather, son, and brother. Since that horrific moment, I've used nearly every ounce of energy to rebuild a life with purpose, pushing forward to prevent as many people as possible from making the wrong choices and mistakes that I've made, especially around drunk driving. There is much more to life than me staying sober. This second life I've been given is so much bigger than me. There is more to life, and I'm on my journey to find it even in my daily habits.

I believe most people fail to realize that purpose can be found in the smallest of actions and the smallest of moments. Every day, I live with purpose and intent to make the right choices. There is a cognizant action made daily to pursue my purpose. It starts with my choices for my life and career the moment I get out of bed. I give thanks to God and then decide what I need to do each day with purpose behind it. When you break life down into the minutia, analyzing the small details, purpose should be broken down into finding meaning in every choice you make and every action that follows. When your intent is to fully live with purpose, and you intend to fight for it no matter the struggle or roadblocks in your way, great things follow. An intentional focus and belief in a second life is why I've changed. There is a greater purpose, but I also find purpose behind the daily choices I make, and that makes a huge difference.

STUMBLING TO PURPOSE

As I sat in the back of the college classroom, an outlandish idea sprang to my mind for the final presentation of the year. At the time, I was enrolled at Front Range Community College for my sixth different year (1999–2003, 2009–2011), the eighth different semester spanning over a twelve-year period at the same campus. Let's just say it felt like my second home. I spent more time in the admissions office than a pre-medical student spends practicing in an operating room. The worst part about it is I never even received an associate's degree from this community college spanning those twelve years.

This last semester was different. I was on a mission when I nervously approached the professor with the idea after everyone had left the classroom. "Professor, can I make the final project something different?" The professor quickly looked up from her computer screen as a curiousness began forming on her face. The professor was the only one in the class who had a vague idea of the situation I was in. She knew I was living at the halfway house and had recently been released from my incarceration. She knew I was back in school trying to get my life together. I pitched my idea to her on my final project. After a few moments of pondering, she nodded in approval. I knew I had a unique class project ahead of me.

Fast forward to the last day of class. The professor called out, "Mr. Fisher, you are up next. It's our last presentation for the semester. It better be a good one." After making eye contact, the professor gave me the slow gesture of acknowledgment as I anxiously got out of my chair, legs shaking, weak, and nearly paralyzed with fear. Little did I know that a glimpse into my future was about to take place in her classroom. Hearing my name called out loud gave me goosebumps. This was different, way different than any of the times before when I was too afraid to speak in front of a group. I was happy and thrilled to be in college again. I was no longer stuck inside of prison walls with barbwire fences or correctional offers checking on me hourly. Excitement and the thrill of learning were motivating me this go-around in school. I was on a path of doing something great, I could feel it, yet I had no idea what it was. I was about to present to the class of eighteen to twenty-year-old freshmen and sophomores who had not lived life yet. They were in for something special. They were going to be my test guinea pigs for the start of a new career I had no intention of ever doing. Heck, I never even knew the words "keynote speaker" existed at the time, but this was going to be my first taste.

After hours of preparation and practice, a calming sense of confidence was protecting me as I walked my way to the front of the small classroom. Plugging my thumb drive into the computer, my hands began to sweat, my body shaking in fear. I took a deep breath to quell my social anxiety before it turned into a full-on panic attack. I gripped the podium to stabilize my body. If I didn't get a hold of my anxiety, I was going to bomb the final presentation. There are times when my panic attacks get so bad, I'll abruptly leave a social or networking event and go hide in a bathroom stall or sit in my car in the parking lot until the event is done. Once the event finishes, I'll go back in at the end to say thank you to the people who invited me and get out of the building as fast as I can. I didn't have this option for this presentation. My grades and unseen future were depending on this exact moment. I closed my eyes and took a deep breath like Will Ferrell does in the movie *Old School.* I blacked out, and everything I practiced came flowing out of my mouth. Halfway through the presentation, I saw tears falling from the young ladies in the front of the classroom. I glanced toward the back rows where all the tough eighteen to twenty-year-old men are, and they couldn't even look me in the eyes. The emotions of my presentation were making an impact.

After finishing my "first" speech for a community college classroom, something clicked. I found something special. What I discovered at that moment was my *purpose* in life. It was my why and what I needed to do for my life's ambitious change to do right in this world. I wouldn't pursue this career until years down the road, but this was the moment that had started it all.

TEACHING PURPOSE

Every year, the minds of millions of students sit behind uncomfortable desks, trying to avoid getting in trouble. They are trained to regurgitate what they are taught. Students are learning the basics of math, speaking, spelling, reading, and writing, and all the necessary tools to have an educated life. This is the case for the kids who are fortunate enough to even go to school, while millions of other youthful minds never receive the opportunity for an education due to where they live or their socioeconomic status. Education is critical for success, but not all people thrive in a traditional education system. Teaching others how to find their passions and purpose should be a foundational brick in everyone's upbringing, no matter the school or lack of schooling a youth may receive.

Everyone who lives and breathes on this earth has a purpose. I believe that. It's the educators', influencers', and parents' job to help the youth learn how to find those purposes. Yet, the vast majority don't. We should be teaching kids to chase their dreams while their brains are still young and malleable, when they still have the youthful exuberance to explore, to be creative before they begin to compare themselves to others—ruining their drive or willingness to step out and be who they truly want to be. We should allow them to follow their dreams and not stifle their visions.

While growing up, school didn't matter to me. Sports was the only thing that brought a sense of purpose to my life. Sports saved my life as a kid. It was more than the game. There is a bigger purpose behind athletics. Athletics creates friendships, it develops work ethics, and it teaches the athlete how to handle being critiqued and criticized by their coach, much like a boss will do to an employee when an individual hits the real world. Sports provide a sense of purpose in lives. It doesn't matter if it's to score their first goal in a soccer game or make the football team, thus making new friends. Sports provide an educational way to deal with adversity, build resiliency, and learn how to communicate. Athletes know how to handle adversity.

THEY'RE ALL GOING TO LAUGH AT YOU

My childhood was in the 1980s and 1990s. Childhood was about as simple and easy as could be, yet it felt like the entire world was conspiring against me. At times, I loathed my family, hated school, detested being around other students, and abhorred being in the hallways surrounded by others. At the drop of a hat, my heart would start racing, my mind doing the same, bracing for the panic from the big, bad, and scary monster of people in groups in the hallway. Little did I know, these were a result of my social anxiety, and I had them often in between class breaks. On the outside, nobody had a clue. I was constantly lying about how I felt inside. Those moments of anxiety and stress seemed to flee and vanish when that orange bouncing Wilson basketball touched my hands. My anxiety and the fear of people also seemed to vanish when my headphones played those beats, lyrics, and rhyming patterns of Tupac, Kid 'n Play, or some other rap artists my parents wanted to be banned. Those energetic sounds reverberated off my big ears, bringing the eardrums inside of me alive. Yet, I was told I could never follow these dreams of basketball and rap music. My parents preached education and schooling. Their idea of purpose was to graduate high school, go to college, get a degree, work a 9–5, have a white picket fence, and start a family. That's how they were raised—no fault of their own, but that is never what I wanted. Yet they kept pushing that life over and over, slowly eroding my dreams to nothing. The two dreams and passions in my life, basketball and hip-hop, were outside of the schooling parameters, so I was never met with positive influence to chase those dreams. Besides, I was tiny, so there was no way I could play basketball. I was about as white as Elmer's glue, and hip-hop was not a part of my culture.

Friends, family, and even my teachers made fun of my dreams. They all laughed at my goal to play in the NBA. What a great way to suppress hopes and dreams as they joked about it to my face. Parents yelling at me to "grow the fuck up and get a real life." Here's one of my favorite quotes I heard often from those who were supposedly supposed to believe in me: "You live in a fantasy world." After all this negative support, I began becoming angry at the world. This was about the time when my anger began brewing and boiling inside. Regrettably, instead of using my anger in a positive manner, I went left, far from right, allowing the dark side of anger to lead the way. I began disliking everyone, even my friends. I began feeling more isolated, never really connecting with many friends. Most of my friendships were only superficial. This led to the depression and self-medicating. At the time, I didn't realize those choices around alcohol and drugs would ruin my life. I started out drinking to socialize, making these superficial friendships that would mean relatively nothing in my adult life. I didn't want to start out drinking and become an alcoholic. I didn't do my first pill of ecstasy thinking I would later fiend for weed, coke, or any pill I could get my hands on. When I became addicted is when my friends and family had every right to utter these sentiments above. I was beyond lazy during the years I was an alcoholic and constantly high, and I never worked hard at anything. But my dreams were crushed before I began drinking, way before I began getting high. Those were after years of being told I couldn't achieve my dream of playing basketball.

Growing up, I was never pushed to dream about life. I was pushed toward a 9–5 and never having gigantic grandiose visions that motivated me to push forward. There were no visions or dreams in my household. I believe everyone should be chasing the dreams and visions you see in your mind. There is nothing wrong with being trapped in an office cubical, working 9–5, or working a manual labor job. Some people are risk-adverse and don't want to gamble with their lives, yet they wake up every day dreading life, asking themselves *Is this my purpose? Is this what I was meant to be?* Their internal dialogue says they hate their life and wish they had a different one. If that's the case for you, it's time to reevaluate where you are. It's more than likely you made a choice to take the easy way out. Chasing your dreams and finding your purpose is difficult. To obtain them, you must sacrifice and work hard. It will be extremely difficult to live the life you want. Understand that you are at this exact moment due to the choices you have made leading up to reading these pages. There have been countless situations and scenarios leading up to this moment where you could have chased your dreams and chased your purpose. Heck, if you have read this far and have not decided to work toward your dreams, I feel like I kind of failed you.

FINDING MY PURPOSE CHANGED EVERYTHING IN MY LIFE

My dream was to play professional basketball overseas, come back home, and invest in real estate like my high school coach did. It was the only thing I consistently imagined and wanted to do from the fourth grade until the age of thirty-four (minus the real estate part;

that dream began in high school). I chased basketball everywhere I could. A self-described vagabond, a hooping nomad. Traveling from school to school, avoiding all friendships, long-term relationships, and connections. It was never a plan to live in one place, settle down, raise a family, or get married. I was a dreamer, often living in a world far away from my reality. Nobody else sees it, but I do.

Prison and the prison boot camp were the best things that happened to my life between the ages of twenty-four and twenty-eight. Being released from prison gave me a new life. It was the best way to start over—as crazy as that sounds. I was given a do-over. Not many people get a do-over, and I did. After prison, I had the ability to start my life over, and I would. I began intently focusing on achieving the things I wanted. I made a choice in prison that I would give basketball another shot, and this time I would do all the things I didn't do at my five previous attempts at college basketball, like being sober, getting decent grades, doing workouts, and lifting weights. By putting on my blinders and focusing on the task at hand, I was going to be vigilant in chasing my goal to take basketball as far as I could. I was one long flight and one decision away from finishing my dream of playing professional basketball. At the time, I didn't care if it was an overseas league that was below the talent of a rec-center here in the States. I didn't care if I had to sleep on floors or get paid in free food or local tail. My dream would have been fulfilled. Yet, I never realized my dreams, and it will go down as one of the three biggest regrets in my life that I still think about every day.

Before the do-over stage of my life, I let others influence me. I let alcohol, drugs, and my mental health influence me. Worst of all, I influenced myself!!! Nobody is to blame for me never achieving my dreams but me. I wasn't strong enough mentally. I wasn't strong enough to have faith in myself because I was doing it wrong. Today, I have *faith* in the choices I make. I will not be stopped from accomplishing the dreams I have. I have *faith* in the purpose and goals for the future I envision. I'm in control of the outcome. Nobody else but *me*.

I had a purpose of finishing my basketball career, and I had no idea that it would lead to my true purpose and calling of being a preventative, story-telling keynote speaker. Life began to adjust and change when I found speaking. I've determined it is the reason why I'm still alive. I found that my choices led to a life with purpose. It created a life I needed but didn't realize I could have.

CALL TO ACTION

PART 1.

List five basic tasks you do on a daily basis. I'll only use these three as examples:

- Paying your bills
- Waking up on time
- Showing up to work early

Now, list those same three tasks followed by a deeper meaning, asking yourself, "Why is this task important in my life?"

Paying your bills: I pay my bills to keep my lights on and my phone charged. I pay my car note because I like having a car to get around town with.

Waking up on time: When I wake up on time, I have no need to feel stressed and rushed to get to work.

Showing up to work early: My boss likes it when I show up earlier than normal. It gives me a good rapport with upper management.

PART 2.

Rewrite the list with those same tasks, but spend time thinking of an even deeper meaning and purposeful intent behind each task. Ask yourself, "How can I use this prior, somewhat meaningless task to become greater?"

Paying your bills: I want to build my credit score so I can buy a house, then invest some of my money so I can buy three investment properties in the future. I pay my bills on time, so I'll never experience getting turned down for a high-interest-rate car loan at a shady car dealership.

Waking up on time: I want an extra ten minutes to do pushups and meditate every morning to help my mind and body get healthier so I can live longer. I also want to be active when I'm old and grey. Getting up early allows more time for me to get ready, and I can decrease the levels of stress I have in the mornings. Ultimately, this will allow me to live longer.

Showing up to work early: I want to show people I'm a leader. I want to outperform the competition. I want to prove to my boss I'm dependable. But even more importantly, I want to be promoted. I have a vision and dream to start my own company. Showing up to this job early will build healthy habits to create my own life, the one I see in my dreams. How can I own my own company if I'm not willing to show up to my current job and do the little things to separate myself from my coworkers?

When you break down small daily tasks, adding deeper meaning and purpose behind them, life will change. There is a purpose behind everything we do. It's up to you to recognize those small purposes and attack them as if they were your larger goals in life. Life's purposes can be found in the details. You must look, recognize, and apply the purpose behind the small things. This leads to your bigger purposes in life that will eventually present themselves.

CHAPTER 24

WISHING I COULD CHANGE THE PAST

My life would be vastly different if I would have just asked for help with my mental health in middle school—when I was young, unaware, uneducated, and overall scared about nearly everything in my life at the time. I had no idea about the options for help in this mental health battle. My choices as a pre-teen were the beginning of many downfalls, including the future pain I would cause others. If I had one single moment of feeling safe, maybe one moment of strength to feel vulnerable, asking for help in middle school, that moment might have prevented the alcohol and drug benders of my past. Getting help in middle school could have helped prevent my future divorce and, more importantly, the accident.

I wish I had never chosen to drink my junior year in high school. This would have altered my entire life. If I had just gone home after losing to Fort Collins High School in 1997 instead of being angry and going out to a party, life would be drastically different. Maybe I wouldn't have developed a taste for alcohol. My anger and emotions influenced my decision to drink. I have a tendency to make impulsive decisions when I'm emotionally revved up. Somewhere along the line, I went from a personal philosophy of "I'll never drink" as a kid to "I'll drink every day."

Do I blame my friends? No, but I know peer pressure was involved. Prior to my first night of drinking, I had been asked many times to drink, yet never did. Deep down, I knew I didn't want to be like my grandmother who died of alcoholism and lung cancer from booze and cigarettes. Eventually, the combination of depression, anger, and being influenced by peer pressure finally dug its nails into me my junior year. It finally broke me, and I surrendered to the temptation and misery of alcohol.

Over the years, I've spent countless hours reflecting on my life, weighing the consequences of my past choices with my current and future choices. It's sad and depressing to realize all the mistakes I've made. I'm a heavily flawed man. Life changed on that horrible day in 2003. Out of the pain and darkness, a new mentality has risen like a phoenix from the ashes. I've had these three little words tattooed on my leg: HOPE, FAITH, and GOD. These three terms, concepts, or philosophies have been applied to my life, pushing me in the right direction.

It's uncomfortable when students ask the question, "Are you a better person now than you were before the accident?" A reluctant and often sad reply of, "Yes, I am," escapes my mouth. It's always difficult admitting this. The truth is, I am a better person now than before the accident. I carried the guilt of the accident and never forgave myself until 2018. From 2003–2018, the extremely heavy burden of Bill's death weighed on me. But, in 2018, an overwhelming feeling that God had forgiven me took hold in my soul. Life has been different since that moment in February of 2018.

One of my hopes is that Bill's family will read this book and come to the conclusion that I've done nearly as much as I can to change the past for the better. I hope they'll realize I'm far from that person I was before 2003. All the amazing work I've done speaking doesn't make up for what I've caused—not at all. No matter how hard I work at changing the world, it won't bring Bill back. Day after day, I make conscious decisions to change, trying to lead a better life. My life is built around preventing others from experiencing the horrific pain I caused. I have a level of commitment and dedication to saving as many lives as possible that very few will ever reach. In truth, I lost my marriage over this speaking career. Speaking and impacting lives will continue to be the priority in my life. I lost my best friend and wife because my focus was on prevention/speaking and not her. She was not a priority—saving lives was. I try to justify that it's part of my universal punishment, but I know that's not the case. Besides, that's not a healthy view to have. Frankly, I ruined Bill's wife's life, and I ruined my life with my wife. I'm sorry to both of you.

During these past two decades, I have heard and seen many others who committed a DUI vehicular homicide who never change. They are still drinking, and some are even drinking and driving. Nearly two decades ago, I made a promise that I *won't* be one of them. I made a promise to God and Bill's family (unknowingly to them) that I will never drink again. Nineteen-plus years later, I've stuck to that promise. I pray that one day Bill's family forgives me of my heinous crime.

CALL TO ACTION

Biggest challenge of all.

This will be the most difficult and humbling challenge in this book. Accomplishing this challenge can release years of stress, years of burden, and take the weight of the world off your shoulders. Wouldn't it be amazing to lose ten pounds instantly? Forgiveness can shed pounds off that you've been burdened with carrying for months, years, and even decades. I know it did for me.

Forgiving somebody who has misled or harmed you takes strength. It takes courage to address something so raw, a pain or torture that has been eating you alive inside. Letting go of that parasitic, unforgiving creature inside, a tapeworm of self-destructive emotional baggage, is cathartic if you allow it to be so. A new layer of life, a new layer of hope and energy will present itself.

I challenge you to forgive yourself. I challenge you to forgive a

loved one or a friend who you've been struggling with. When I truly
believed that God forgave me (more in the closing chapter), my life became lighter. The weight of the accident and Bill's death will always be
carried. I can't forget what happened, nor do I ever want to. As a matter
of fact, I have Bill's name tattooed on my right arm. Every day when I
brush my teeth or flex my wanna-be biceps in the mirror to boost my
fragile ego, a dose of reality hits as I realize my past. I've forgiven myself for the accident but didn't do so until 2018. When you break free
with forgiveness, amazing things can happen.

- Make a list of five people about whom you carry emotional
  weight. List them in order from the least painful to the most
  painful. Start with the least painful person you want to forgive
  and let them know how you feel. Be vulnerable. I don't care if
  you are a man or woman, old or young, right or left side of the
  political line, but be open and honest. Honesty and vulnerability
  will create emotional bonds between you both. Tell the person
  how you feel. Get it off your chest.

- Make your way down the list, building confidence before ap-
  proaching the hardest person to forgive. This will allow you a
  trial by fire of what works and doesn't work as you work your
  way down your list.

- Hopefully, after four successful, meaningful conversations about
  your relationships with those individuals on the list, the hardest
  and final member on your list will be easier.

Here's a second option.

- You can rip the bandage off quickly and go to the person who
  has hurt you the worst and let it all air out. This is not easy. It
  will be painful. It more than likely will bring up the past and
  deep-seated emotions that have been brewing underneath the
  surface since the moment you felt wronged. You will ultimately

feel better about yourself because you are taking care of your foundation, your mental, emotional, and social health. Not every attempt to talk to somebody will work. Believe me, when I did this process on a few of the people on my list, they didn't care. It didn't work on of them. But guess what? I'm at peace and feel significantly better. I'm happy I tried, even if it didn't turn out the way I wanted it to. The key is I tried, so it's no longer on me to harbor that pain. It's on them now.

This book is intended to be a starting brick in the foundation of building a better you. It's not a magic pill that will make life perfect. This book is built from my experiences and harmful actions, but applying these parts and maintaining my foundation continue to help me become who I am today. I'm far from perfect, but I'm comfortable with who I am and what I've been through. Yes, I could have made better choices recently with certain business and personal decisions, but the key is, I'm moving forward each day. The biggest gains came after the hardest work. Seeking, searching, and finding forgiveness changed the game. I believe it can help you as well.

CHAPTER 25

FORGIVENESS—BILL'S STORY

On the last day of February 2018, I entered the auditorium and met with the technical point of contact for my presentation slides and microphone for a school keynote. He was an older gentleman with a full head of hair. We briefly exchanged pleasantries during the set-up of my PowerPoint and quick audio sound check. The man asked what the speech was about, and I replied with my typical blanket statement about a preventative message using stories of my life. He politely responded that he had no plans to stay for the speech. Not thinking much more of it, I went about my business of testing my microphone and keynote slide deck.

Mind you, this was the first speech I had ever given to a private Christian middle and high school. My nerves and butterflies were on high alert, more so than other events, in part due to the professional setup of the stage. The stage had multiple-colored lights above, pointed directly at the stage like most auditoriums across the country, but this was a more complex setup. It was filled with musical equipment that was played for the school events and their Sunday services. The stage was surrounded by plexiglass with massive TVs mounted at various focal points of the room, all facing the stadium seats aimed at the stage. It felt like a Sunday sermon you would see on a regional television broadcast for tens of thousands of believers and worshipers. This was a new and unique stage setup that influenced the impact of my speech. I felt like a true professional speaker, even though I'd been a paid speaker for the four years prior. This was a bigger production, and it added to my nerves. I was on stage in a church feeling like a pastor preaching to his flock. It was a powerful feeling.

Following my speech, a line of students waited to speak to me, like most events. After finishing with the students, I went to the production booth to grab my flash drive and remote clicker. The tech guy with grey hair, grey beard, and glasses, who was the first person to greet me at the door upon checking into the school building, said, "I don't know why, but I had this feeling I needed to stay and watch your event. Something was burning inside that told me I needed to watch your event and to speak with you." Various confused thoughts rushed through my cerebral cortex and grey matter. Where might this conversation be heading? Was he about to be critical of my career? It wouldn't be the first time people had criticized me—and it probably wouldn't be the last. His response would be a moment in my life I'll never forget.

He uttered the most profound statement that changed my life. "My name is Bill, and I'm fifty-seven years old—and Bill forgives you."

This man shook me to my core. He had all the same features as Bill (from the accident), with his beard, glasses, and grey hair, and he was the same exact age.

Instantly, I was locked deeply into this man's eyes, staring intensely into his soul. He was doing the same. There was a silence that seemed to overtake the building. Goosebumps on my arms, neck, and chest began to rise from my skin the size of the Himalayan mountains. The flat skin, rumbling to the peak and zenith of maximum height from the largest organ in the body, began shivering and burning on fire at the same time. Thousands of responses entered my mind, but I stumbled over elementary words and any ability to commence a dialogue. I'd already had a conversation with this gentleman, so why couldn't I find the words to speak? Sound wouldn't escape my thin lips and dry mouth. A brain filled with several degrees of formal education could only muster a simple "Wow." In a life-changing moment, all I could produce was a three-lettered, one-syllable word that toddlers regurgitate with ease and regularity, "*Wow.*"

A gigantic ear-to-ear smile dawned on my face as tears began to pool up in my eyes. They started pouring from my eyes and down my cheeks. This was a stranger I had briefly met only two hours before, but we hugged each other as tight as possible, in an embrace that family members who haven't seen one another for years would be jealous of. At that moment, Bill was the closest person in my world. We embraced, we hugged, we cried with purpose. To me, nothing else mattered.

Upon separation from this momentous embrace, Bill looked directly into me, piercing my soul, and repeated:

"Bill forgives you."

Life has never been the same since that winter day in 2018. My professionalism as a speaker shifted. All the harbored shame, guilt, self-loathing, personal disgust, and self-hate seemed to vanish. Instant forgiveness overtook my body—and nothing has changed my speaking career more so than that very moment. This experience altered this journey to help others through my story, awareness, prevention, and inspiration. Finally, I knew at this point I could authentically and genuinely allow forgiveness to enter my life. This confirmed my purpose.

Standing on stage and hosting one-on-one or small group discussions in libraries after my events is my *why*. Spending hours emailing or messaging students after my events is my *why*. Speaking to schools, students, parents, adults, communities, prisons, camps, and corporations was all confirmed as my purpose on this day. This was my calling, and I understood through the heavenly ether that Bill approved.

"Thank you," was all I could utter after our deep embrace. At that moment, my elated mind attempted to fully grasp and recognize the moment for what it was. I couldn't grasp the entire significance of what it meant. It was a sensory overload, blasting off to an entirely new level of energy and enthusiasm. Never had my mind and body reached this level of vibration and frequency before. This was an entirely new out-look on life. A defining moment in my life to make this world better. This moment was *life-changing.*

"The world works in mysterious ways" is a term we've all heard. A man I'd never met before, and had never spoken to before that day, changed the rest of my life! This grey-haired, older gentleman provid-ed a sense of relief and forgiveness from a black cloud that had en-gulfed my life for fifteen years. An incalculable weight was lifted off my body and mind. I felt free. I felt free from the pressure, free from the guilt about being a professional speaker. A powerful boost of pos-itive energy and sense of freedom filled my soul. I had more energy and excitement than my first day in the halfway house after being in-carcerated for three years. The guilt and shame I carried when I got out of prison was lifted. The dense fog that followed me during every move and breath when I left the halfway house and transitioned to the DOC's intensive supervision program (ISP) was lifted and vanished into thin air. On this day, I had more faith and freedom than the day I signed my Department of Corrections release papers when my brother laughed at me during my jubilant jumping spree off the furniture. I was running around our house screaming at the top of my lungs, "I'm free. I'm fucking free. I'm free!!!" No more daily check-in calls to the DOC, no more calling my color line. There wouldn't be any more threats of going back to prison for a parole violation, which had always been a possibility if my parole officer was having a bad day and wanted to be a jerk. The brick walls, armed guards, ankle monitor, parole officer meetings, piss tests, and breathalyzers—all gone. The small possibility of a stupid violation was no more. None of that was as significant to my life as "My name is Bill, and I'm fifty-seven years old. Bill forgives you!"

I was free to live life again, become a new person, and change the world, all stemming from a short conversation and the simple words… which I'm going to repeat one more time: "My name is Bill, and I'm fifty-seven years old. Bill forgives you!"

That was February 28th, 2018.

ACKNOWLEDGMENTS

There are times I find myself on stage in complete disbelief of my own story, often shaking my head, thinking of all the opportunities I've had and the choices I've made, leading me to that exact moment in life. Frankly, I don't know how I'm still alive and breathing, yet I am. I never imagined becoming a keynote speaker and now an author. Since fourth grade, my only goal in life was basketball. I always thought my life plan would be to play hoops and coach, train, or work in a basketball front office. Life handed me a much different path, so here I am, changing the lives of hundreds of thousands of people. It's the best job in the world.

First and foremost, I thank *God*. Since the horrific night in 2003, at the lowest imaginable moment, *God* had been the footsteps carrying me through life. I'm nothing without. Secondly, my family. You were the support I needed in the past to get through some of the darkest and most challenging times after the accident. Our family grew closer and tighter during those rough years, but life has pulled us all in different directions, drastically changing our family dynamics. I will always love and appreciate all of you.

Now, on to my thank yous. Some will think they are completely absurd and off-base. It's my life, my thank yous, and my damn book.

If you don't like it, too bad. I don't care. I must give my love and appreciation for the game of basketball. That globe-shaped ball saved my life more than anything in this world. I wouldn't be here if not for that orange bouncing thing—a true lifesaver. You were my one true love that gave me a reason to wake up every day. To the GOAT, R.I.P. Tupac and the world of hip-hop music—in the grips of the grim reaper, rap was always there—giving me the strength and energy to keep fighting. These four (*God*, family, hoops, and hip-hop) have been my biggest foundations and pillars of influence during my times of need when nothing or nobody else mattered. All saved my life at some point, and I wouldn't be writing this line without their impact. Thank you.

This is my opportunity to shout-out some other impactful people who had influence, or I consider deserving of recognition from moments that aided me through rough waters. This will catch some people off guard, maybe offend some people, especially when I list the most influential people in my life. Are you ready?

I never wanted to be anyone I ever met. I never wanted to be average, work a 9–5, or have a regular job. Every day of my youth, from seventh grade on, my greatest influences were basketball and rap music—hands down. Tupac, Eminem, Allen Iverson, and Jason Williams (a.k.a. White Chocolate) were the only four people I ever wanted to be. (There was a few-year period when I wanted to drink and party like Jimmy Buffet.) Those four pushed me every day in the gym, every day in school when I hated life, every day in prison, and every day after until I was roughly thirty-six years of age. I'm who I am because I grew up emulating them. Heck, I even have tattoos due to them. Are they the best role models in the world's eyes? Not likely, but they are a major reason for my internal strength and surviving through all that I have.

Now on to real life. :)

The two grown men I would have run through a brick wall for. First, Coach Jim Noonan. Coach, if it wasn't for you, I would have headed down the wrong path. I became the basketball player I was due to your coaching and you not allowing me to get away with anything.

Coach Jeff Culver, I'm a success story because of you. You gave me a storybook opportunity to finish not only my basketball career but all my college degrees.

Thank you to all my college coaches who gave me all the shots I screwed up. Thank you to all the basketball players and men at the Fort Collins Club, all the Sunday Hoops (Hawes) and Northside crews. Thank you to all my teammates over the years—I can't list them all out, as I've had more teammates than most.

The "GUY" will always be grateful to Micah for a couch to crash on when I was homeless with my counterpart Z, my vet PG. To my other PG, B-Wabbitt, the only dude I could flow with, but more importantly, you gave me a place to stay upon release. Bfunk, you were there after the accident for my bros (and mom's food), but more importantly, you up and moved your life to move in with me when I got released. Antwon, you have been a true friend, one of the only people to write to me in prison. You wrote to me when you were playing pro ball from other countries—that's a true friend! Nate L, my bro. You let me stay at your place when I couldn't find housing as a convicted felon. You, my friend, helped push my story to what it is now. Without you at JWU, I wouldn't have this story. My JWU squad, you sacrificed for me, and we changed that program together. Soup Sauce, little bro, you were the best roommate I could have asked for. S. McGee, all the driving, rebounding, and time in the gym together, much appreciated. Bakeshow, beatboxing in the weight room, and all the Ari moments, my friend.

To President Betty M, you allowed me to flourish on campus with the help of what I called my Trio of leaders—Professor Gilbert, Meredith, and Vander Kooi. I learned so much from all of you. My future success is, in part, because of your education and wisdom. Marcel P., you took a chance on me as a mentee—I will always be grateful. You also introduced me to Tommy. Tommy, thank you for showing me the potential in this career and opening up your home when I lost everything. Bemo, thanks for your positive influence and being there at a time when nobody else was. Jerry M., you kept my purpose and career going due to your generosity.

For you all below, I hope you read this book. To all my boys during my luxurious (sarcastic joke) stay in the DOC, I was motivated to succeed so you could witness that it could actually be done the right way. My hope was always to prove to you that you don't have to go back to that vicious trap and cycle of recidivism. Tank, I miss you, big homie. RR (a.k.a. T2), I see you working on staying out—keep it up. Levi and Slim, hope life is great. Tino, I dropped one of your nuggets of wisdom in here, foo.

Matt, my baby bro. We had an amazing ride together for over a decade. I miss those days, but life hit us both. You're a pops now!

Liz, the best three years of my life. I'm sorry and wish I would have handled things differently.

My puppies. Dizzle, Penny, and Farley. You literally saved my life, my best friends!

To Bill's family, this is obviously not a thank you but a dedication to you. I made a promise to *God* and to Bill to change and change for the better. I've worked tirelessly to do so. Does it make up for the fact that Bill is no longer here? *No*, not at all. I've dedicated my life to changing, aiding, altering, educating, inspiring, and impacting as many people as I can so they never make the mistakes that I have. I pray for you every morning and night.

ENDNOTES

CHAPTER 4

1   "Small Business Statistics." Chamber Of Commerce, 6 Nov. 2023, https://www. chamberofcommerce.org/small@business@statistics/.

2   Crawford, Greg. "Depression Rates in US Tripled When the Pandemic First Hit— Now, They're Even Worse." Boston University. October 7, 2021. https://www.bu.edu/ articles/2021/depression-rates-tripled-when-pandemic-first-hit/.

3   Leonhardt, Megan. "What You Need to Know about the Cost and Accessibility of Mental Health Care in America." CNBC. May 10, 2021. https://www.cnbc. com/2021/05/10/cost-and-accessibility-of-mental-health-care-in-america.html.

4   National Alliance on Mental Illness. "Mental Health by the Numbers." March 2021. https://nami.org/mhstats.

5   McFarland, Matt. "Crazy Good: How Mental Illnesses Help Entrepreneurs Thrive." *Washington Post.* April 19, 2015. https://www.washingtonpost.com/news/innovations/ wp/2015/04/29/crazy-good-how-mental-illnesses-help-entrepreneurs-thrive/.

6   DeSimone, Danielle. "Military Suicide Rates Are at an All-Time High; Here's How We're Trying to Help." United Service Organizations. September 1, 2021. https:// www.uso.org/stories/2664-military-suicide-rates-are-at-an-all-time-high-heres-how- were-trying-to-help.

7   "Suicide among Veterans—Why Are Veterans at a Higher Risk of Suicide?" *American Addiction Centers.* September 12, 2023. https://www.americanaddictioncen- ters.org/veterans/suicide-among-veterans.

CHAPTER 5

1   Association for Psychological Science. "Study Finds That People Can Recover and Thrive after Mental Illness and Substance-Use Disorders." April 5, 2022. https://medicalxpress.com/news/2022-04-people-recover-mental-illness-substance-use.html.

2   Abbott, Brianna. "Youth Suicide Rate Increased 56% in Decade, CDC Says." *Wall Street Journal.* October 17, 2019. https://www.wsj.com/articles/youth-suicide-rate-rises-56-in-decade-cdc-says-11571284861.

3   Statista. "U.S. Teens Daily Screen Time by Income 2019." July 7, 2022. https://www.statista.com/statistics/1099629/hours-screen-time-teens-income/.

4   Sullivan, Glenn. "Divorce Is a Risk Factor for Suicide, Especially for Men." *Psychology Today.* June 30, 2019. https://www.psychologytoday.com/us/blog/acquainted-the-night/201906/divorce-is-risk-factor-suicide-especially-men.

CHAPTER 6

1   https://www.alcoholhelp.com/alcohol/the-effects-of-alcohol-abuse/cost-of-alcoholism/.

2   World Health Organization (WHO). "Alcohol." May 9, 2022. https://www.who.int/news-room/fact-sheets/detail/alcohol.

3   Perry, Daryl. "Is Alcohol a Depressant? If So, What Are the Effects?" *USA TODAY.* August 5, 2022. https://www.usatoday.com/story/life/health-wellness/2022/08/05/is-alcohol-depressant-definition/10163737002/.

4   Center for Disease Control and Prevention. "Excessive Alcohol Use: A Drain on the American Economy." December 30, 2019. https://www.cdc.gov/alcohol/onlinemedia/infographics/excessive-alcohol-economy.html.

5   Center for Disease Control and Prevention. "Costs and Expenditures." August 22, 2022. https://www.cdc.gov/tobacco/data_statistics/fact_sheets/fast_facts/cost-and-expenditures.html.

6   Centers for Disease Control and Prevention. "U.S. Overdose Deaths in 2021 Increased Half as Much as in 2020 – but Are Still up 15%." 11 May 2022. www.cdc.gov/nchs/pressroom/nchs_press_releases/2022/202205.htm.

7   https://www.scientificamerican.com/article/our-bodies-replace-billions-of-cells-every-day/#:~:text=About%20330%20billion%20cells%20are%20replaced%20daily%2C%20equivalent,will%20have%20replenished%E2%80%94the%20equivalent%20of%20a%20new%20you.

CHAPTER 7

1 Wang, Yunqiao, Jitender Sareen, Tracie O. Afifi, Shay-Lee Bolton, Edward A. Johnson, James M. Bolton. "Recent Stressful Life Events and Suicide Attempt." *Psychiatric Annals* 42, no. 3 (February 2012): 101–8. https://doi.org/10.3928/00485713-20120217-07.

2 Money and Mental Health Policy Institute. "Money and Mental Health: THE FACTS." https://www.moneyandmentalhealth.org/wp-content/uploads/2017/06/Money-and-mental-health-the-facts-1.pdf.

3 Bond, Nikki, Holkar, Merlyn. "A Silent Killer: Breaking the Link between Financial Difficulty and Suicide." Money and Mental Health. https://www.moneyandmentalhealth.org/wp-content/uploads/2018/12/A-Silent-Killer-Report.pdf.

4 Zapata, Kimberly. "Financial Stress Is a Leading Catalyst for Suicide—These Steps Can Help Save Lives." August 25, 2021. https://www.health.com/money/financial-stress-suicide-risk.

CHAPTER 8

1 "Introducing Tito the Anxiety Mosquito—Big Mouth." Accessed October 13, 2022. https://youtu.be/gM3TB6dvSXo.

2 Broz, Matic. "How Many Photos Are There? 50+ Photos Statistics (2022)." February 17, 2022. https://phototutorial.com/photos-statistics/.

3 Neighmond, Patti. "Of Cigs and Selfies: Teens Imitate Risky Behavior Shared Online." March 10, 2014. https://www.npr.org/sections/health-shots/2014/03/10/258690319/of-cigs-and-selfies-teens-imitate-risky-behavior-shared-online.

4 Sherrell, Zia. "Social Media and Mental Health: Depression and Psychological Effects." September 15, 2021. https://www.medicalnewstoday.com/articles/social-media-and-mental-health#statistics.

5 Centers for Disease Control and Prevention. "Facts about Suicide." January 21, 2021. https://www.cdc.gov/suicide/facts/index.html.

6 Centers for Disease Control and Prevention. "Suicide Data and Statistics." November 29, 2023. https://www.cdc.gov/suicide/suicide-data-statistics.html.

CHAPTER 11

1   Movendi International. "Big Alcohol Exposed: Big Investments in Advertising Onslaught." May 28, 2021. https://movendi.ngo/news/2021/05/28/big-alcohol-exposed-big-investments-in-advertising-onslaught/.

2   World Health Organization. "Alcohol." 9 May 2022. https://www.who.int/news-room/fact-sheets/detail/alcohol.

3   Carlin, Doug. "All 50 US States Ranked by Population [Report 2022]." *USA by Numbers.* April 8, 2021. https://usabynumbers.com/states-ranked-by-population/.

4   "Drunk Driving Arrest Statistics." Accessed October 11, 2022. http://www.drunkdrivingprevention.com/drunkdrivingarreststatistics.html.

5   Centers for Disease Control and Prevention. "Alcohol-Related Deaths." August 3, 2020. https://www.cdc.gov/alcohol/features/excessive-alcohol-deaths.html.

6   USA FACTS.ORG. "US Gun Deaths." 2021. https://usafacts.org/data/topics/security-safety/crime-and-justice/firearms/firearm-deaths/.

7   Center for Disease Control and Prevention. "Excessive Alcohol Use: A Drain on the American Economy." December 30, 2019. https://www.cdc.gov/alcohol/onlinemedia/infographics/excessive-alcohol-economy.html.

8   Mueller, Chris. "Fact Check: Men Accounted for about 80% of US Suicides in 2021." USA Today. 6 Dec. 2022. https://www.usatoday.com/story/news/factcheck/2022/12/06/fact-check-men-accounted-80-us-suicides-2021/10838683002/.

CHAPTER 12

1   Ibid.

2   "Highlights for 2020 National Survey on Drug Use and Health." SAMHSA. 26 Oct. 2021. https://www.samhsa.gov/data/sites/default/files/2021-10/2020_NSDUH_Highlights.pdf.

CHAPTER 13

1   Schwantes, Marcel. "Science Says 92 Percent of People Don't Achieve Their Goals. Here's How the Other 8 Percent Do." Inc. July 26, 2016. https://www.inc.com/marcel-schwantes/science-says-92-percent-of-people-dont-achieve-goals-heres-how-the-other-8-perce.html.

CHAPTER 15

1 "The Harvard MBA Business School Study on Goal Setting." Wanderlust Worker. Accessed 2 Feb. 2024. https://www.wanderlustworker.com/the-harvard-mba-business-school-study-on-goal-setting/.

2 Clifton, Jim. "The World's Broken Workplace." Gallup. June 13, 2017. https://news.gallup.com/opinion/chairman/212045/world-broken-workplace.aspx?g_source=position1&g_medium=related&g_campaign=tiles.

PART 4

1 Centers for Disease Control and Prevention. "Excessive Alcohol Use and Risks to Men's Health." October 31, 2022. https://www.cdc.gov/alcohol/fact-sheets/mens-health.htm.

CHAPTER 19

2 Bruder, Jessica. "The Psychological Price of Entrepreneurship." Inc. August 20, 2013. https://www.inc.com/magazine/201309/jessica-bruder/psychological-price-of-entrepreneurship.html.

CHAPTER 20

1 Brown, Joshua, Joel Wong. "How Gratitude Changes You and Your Brain." Greater Good. June 6, 2017. https://greatergood.berkeley.edu/article/item/how_gratitude_changes_you_and_your_brain.

2 Chowdhury, Madhuleena Roy. "The Neuroscience of Gratitude and How It Affects Anxiety & Grief." PositivePsychology.com. April 9, 2019. https://positivepsychology.com/neuroscience-of-gratitude/.

CHAPTER 21

1 Centers for Disease Control and Prevention. "Underage Drinking." October 26, 2022. https://www.cdc.gov/alcohol/fact-sheets/underage-drinking.htm.

2 "Small Business Statistics." Chamber Of Commerce. November 6 2023. https://www.chamberofcommerce.org/small-business-statistics/